IT'S A *good* LIFE!

Introduction by **Alisa Kwitney**   5

All things by immortal power
near or far,
Hiddenly
To each other linked are,
That thou canst not stir a flower
Without troubling of a star.

ARTHUR QUILLER-COUCH

I think it was Henry James who talked about the "iron curtain of marriage" which falls over a couple, obscuring everything that goes on behind it. Of course, these days many couples are not married, and many more seem to reveal a great deal about their relationships: How often they fight, how frequently they have sex, how seldom they go out to dinner.

Yet still the iron curtain remains, obscuring the heart of the matter. Couples who seem openly bitter, complaining volubly about each other's physical shortcomings, exposing the bloody, raw meat of their dissension, stay together year after implausible year. Infuriatingly contented pairs, smiling smugly as they caress each other's toes, separate one day, suddenly admitting to a long history of conflict.

Relationships are like giant squid: we only get to see inside them after they're dead. And I don't just mean romantic relationships: I mean the platonic kind, too. Despite the fact that our culture tends to depict the platonic relationship as though it were a big, friendly dog, it, too, is really a giant squid. A close friend is not a cheap substitute for a lover. As any ten year old girl can tell you, friendship is in and of itself mysterious, rare, elusive, and multi-tentacled. Friendship is its own kind of romance. It can be brief. It can be broken. It can be betrayed.

Terry Moore knows this. He knows the whole absurd dance of intimacy, in which we spend a certain amount of time deceiving ourselves, and a certain amount of time deceiving the other, while all the time trying to bridge the gap of misunderstanding that divides us. He speaks the language of the unspoken so fluently that he can capture a subtle shift in emotional tense with the smallest of gestures, the simplest of lines.

This is why STRANGERS IN PARADISE is the comic I hand to people — usually women — who have never read a comic, and have no interest whatsoever in superheroes or horror or fantasy. Readers who view comic books as a strange, quirky, campy but slightly shallow medium — the drag queen of literature — are surprised to find that SIP claims as its principal territory the small, densely populated, intensely fertile landscape of relationships. This has long been the province of novels, in which characters can spend fifty pages considering the implications of a glance, and the dramatic possibility of a long-awaited conversation can keep a reader hooked for chapters and chapters.

But because SIP is a comic, and not a novel, it manages to convey all this with a brevity of language that sometimes borders on, and at other times spills over into, poetry. Poetry that manages to co-exist with unapologetic bits of slapstick. Poetry that blends into eloquent silences, or torrents of words that are almost like silences. This last is, I think, a Terry Moore specialty: A perfect example of it is included in the second issue of this collection.

Katchoo and David face each other, and she is furious, desperate, frightened and appalled by his declaration of love for her. Tears streaming down her cheeks, Katchoo yells at David that he is a stupid boy who doesn't really know her, and then her words disappear down, over David's shoulder and out of the confines of her balloon, reappearing in a kind of wailing wall behind them. Are these words spoken? Unspoken? It seems irrelevant. The words are waves in a verbal sea, bricks in a barricade. They spell out the message: If you truly knew me, you could not love me, and therefore your love is false, and I hate you because your love is false.

This is the true heart of romance. And this is why these four issues are probably my very favorites: Because they focus solely on the triangle of Katchoo, Francine, and David and the age-old story of love unrequited, love sort-of requited, and love that might be requited if you play your cards right.

With nothing pressing happening in the sub-plot to distract Terry, he can take his time on tangential bits, tasty raisins in the crumbcake of the story. One such nugget is the scene in which Francine runs into an old friend in the video shop. The moment where the two women first meet is perfectly honest, completely hilarious, and painfully accurate — and demonstrates how well Terry understands people in general and women in particular.

Verbally and visually, he shows us recognizably human characters — female and male, self-conscious, half-conscious, weight-conscious and imperfect — in all their lusty, crazy, idiosyncratic glory. This is a soap opera worth watching, and I, for one, am hooked.

Alisa Kwitney
New York City, 1996

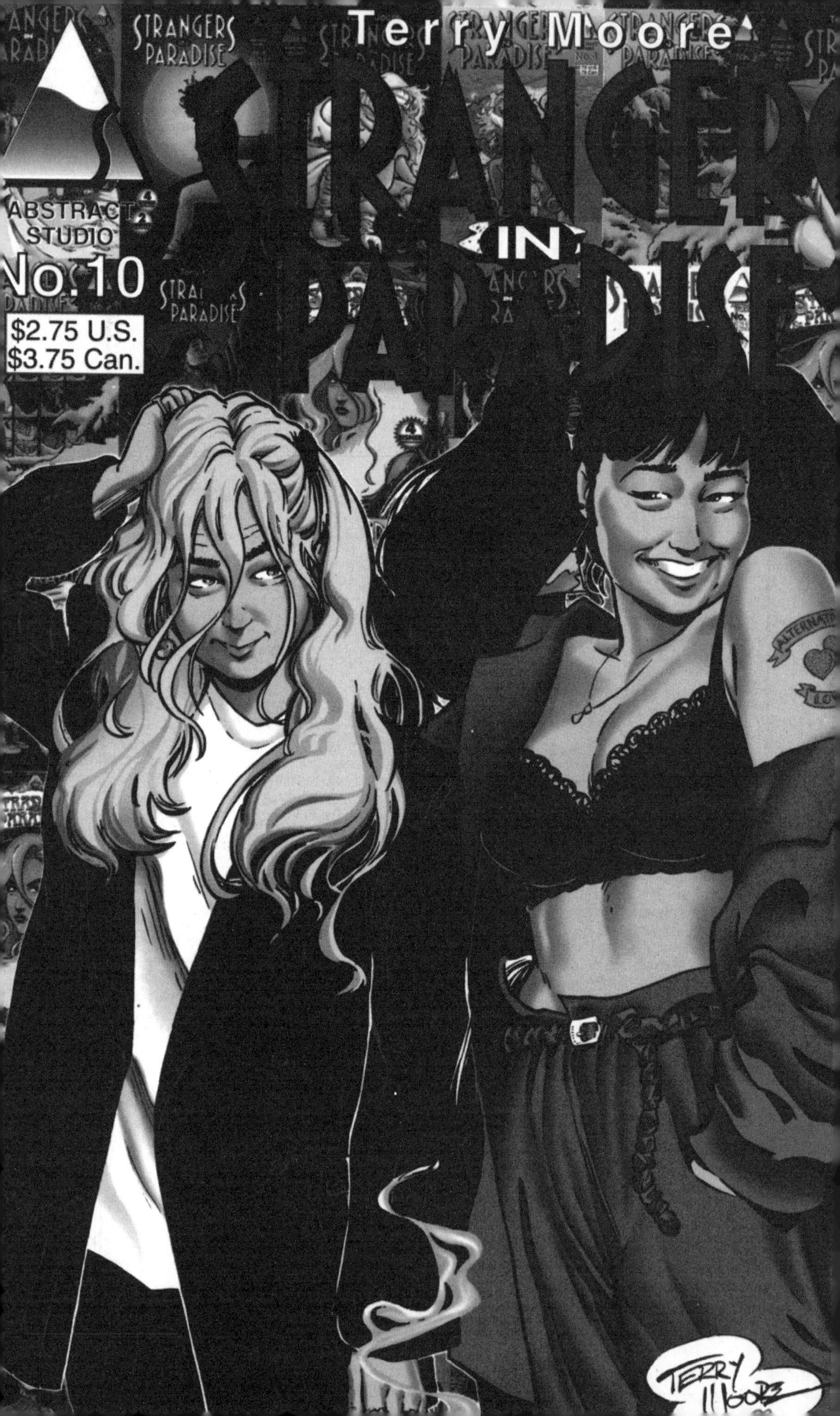
Terry Moore
STRANGERS PARADISE
IN
ABSTRACT STUDIO
No.10
$2.75 U.S.
$3.75 Can.

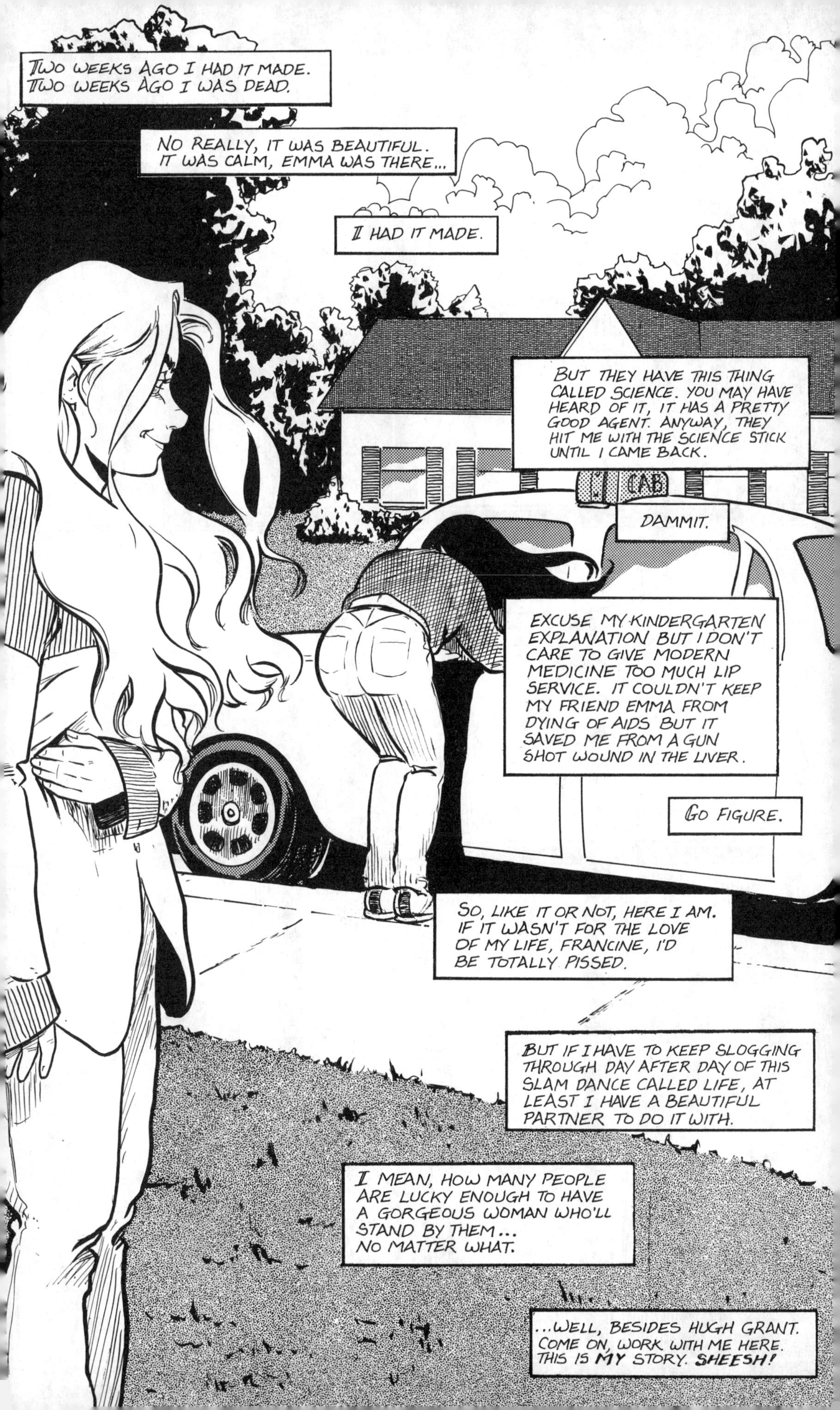
TWO WEEKS AGO I HAD IT MADE. TWO WEEKS AGO I WAS DEAD.
NO REALLY, IT WAS BEAUTIFUL. IT WAS CALM, EMMA WAS THERE...
I HAD IT MADE.
BUT THEY HAVE THIS THING CALLED SCIENCE. YOU MAY HAVE HEARD OF IT, IT HAS A PRETTY GOOD AGENT. ANYWAY, THEY HIT ME WITH THE SCIENCE STICK UNTIL I CAME BACK.
CAB
DAMMIT.
EXCUSE MY KINDERGARTEN EXPLANATION BUT I DON'T CARE TO GIVE MODERN MEDICINE TOO MUCH LIP SERVICE. IT COULDN'T KEEP MY FRIEND EMMA FROM DYING OF AIDS BUT IT SAVED ME FROM A GUN SHOT WOUND IN THE LIVER.
GO FIGURE.
SO, LIKE IT OR NOT, HERE I AM. IF IT WASN'T FOR THE LOVE OF MY LIFE, FRANCINE, I'D BE TOTALLY PISSED.
BUT IF I HAVE TO KEEP SLOGGING THROUGH DAY AFTER DAY OF THIS SLAM DANCE CALLED LIFE, AT LEAST I HAVE A BEAUTIFUL PARTNER TO DO IT WITH.
I MEAN, HOW MANY PEOPLE ARE LUCKY ENOUGH TO HAVE A GORGEOUS WOMAN WHO'LL STAND BY THEM... NO MATTER WHAT.
...WELL, BESIDES HUGH GRANT. COME ON, WORK WITH ME HERE. THIS IS MY STORY. SHEESH!

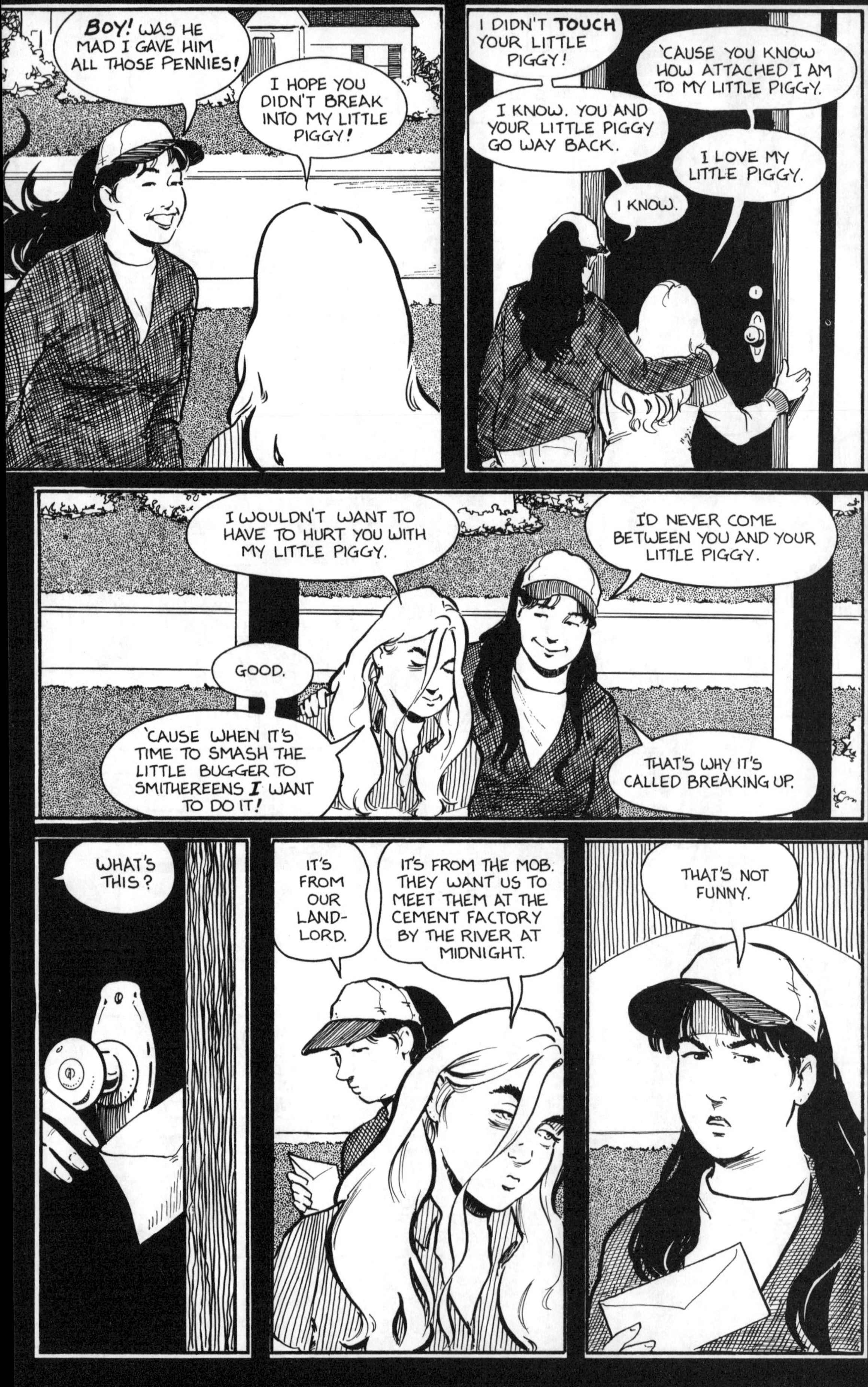
BOY! WAS HE MAD I GAVE HIM ALL THOSE PENNIES!
I HOPE YOU DIDN'T BREAK INTO MY LITTLE PIGGY!
I DIDN'T TOUCH YOUR LITTLE PIGGY!
I KNOW. YOU AND YOUR LITTLE PIGGY GO WAY BACK.
'CAUSE YOU KNOW HOW ATTACHED I AM TO MY LITTLE PIGGY.
I LOVE MY LITTLE PIGGY.
I KNOW.
I WOULDN'T WANT TO HAVE TO HURT YOU WITH MY LITTLE PIGGY.
I'D NEVER COME BETWEEN YOU AND YOUR LITTLE PIGGY.
GOOD.
'CAUSE WHEN IT'S TIME TO SMASH THE LITTLE BUGGER TO SMITHEREENS I WANT TO DO IT!
THAT'S WHY IT'S CALLED BREAKING UP.
WHAT'S THIS?
IT'S FROM OUR LAND-LORD.
IT'S FROM THE MOB. THEY WANT US TO MEET THEM AT THE CEMENT FACTORY BY THE RIVER AT MIDNIGHT.
THAT'S NOT FUNNY.

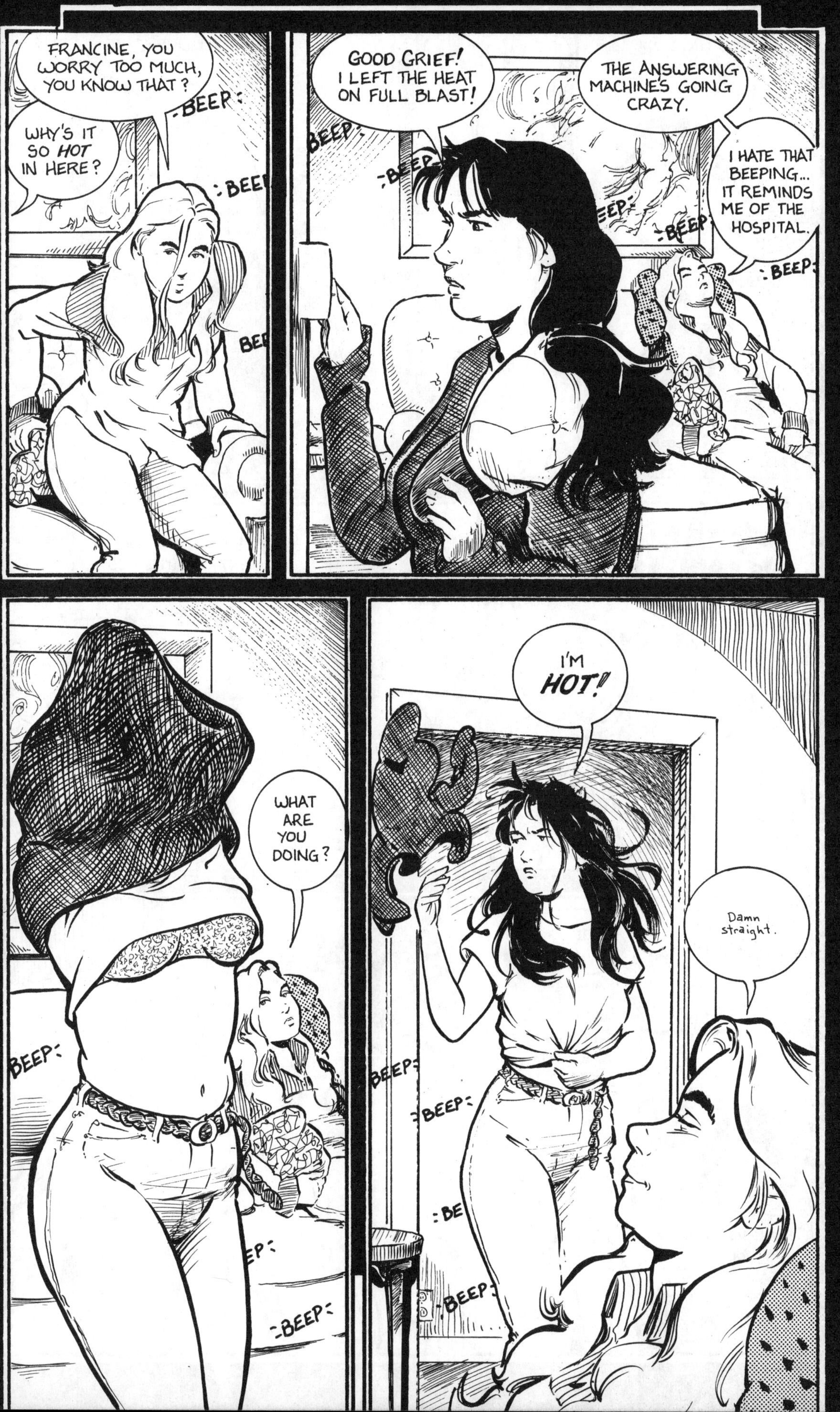

FRANCINE, YOU WORRY TOO MUCH, YOU KNOW THAT?
WHY'S IT SO *HOT* IN HERE?
BEEP
BEEP
GOOD GRIEF! I LEFT THE HEAT ON FULL BLAST!
THE ANSWERING MACHINE'S GOING CRAZY.
I HATE THAT BEEPING... IT REMINDS ME OF THE HOSPITAL.
BEEP
BEEP
BEEP
BEEP
BEEP
WHAT ARE YOU DOING?
BEEP
BEEP
I'M *HOT!*
Damn straight.
BEEP
BEEP
BEEP

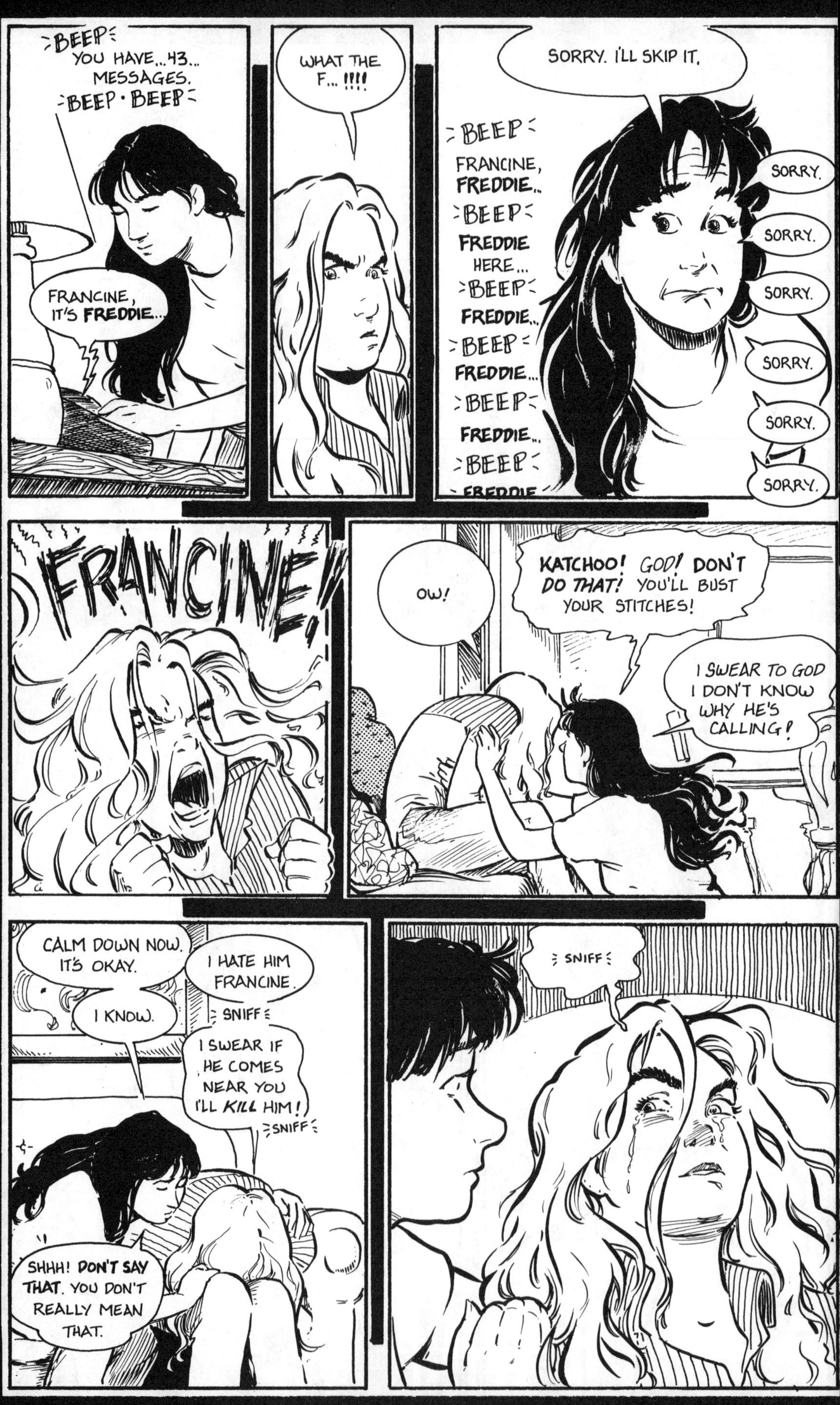
BEEP
YOU HAVE...43... MESSAGES.
BEEP · BEEP
FRANCINE, IT'S FREDDIE...
WHAT THE F... !!!!
SORRY. I'LL SKIP IT.
BEEP
FRANCINE, FREDDIE...
BEEP
FREDDIE HERE...
BEEP
FREDDIE...
BEEP
FREDDIE...
BEEP
FREDDIE...
BEEP
SORRY.
SORRY.
SORRY.
SORRY.
SORRY.
SORRY.
FRANCINE!
OW!
KATCHOO! GOD! DON'T DO THAT! YOU'LL BUST YOUR STITCHES!
I SWEAR TO GOD I DON'T KNOW WHY HE'S CALLING!
CALM DOWN NOW. IT'S OKAY.
I HATE HIM FRANCINE.
I KNOW.
SNIFF
I SWEAR IF HE COMES NEAR YOU I'LL KILL HIM!
SNIFF
SHHH! DON'T SAY THAT. YOU DON'T REALLY MEAN THAT.
SNIFF

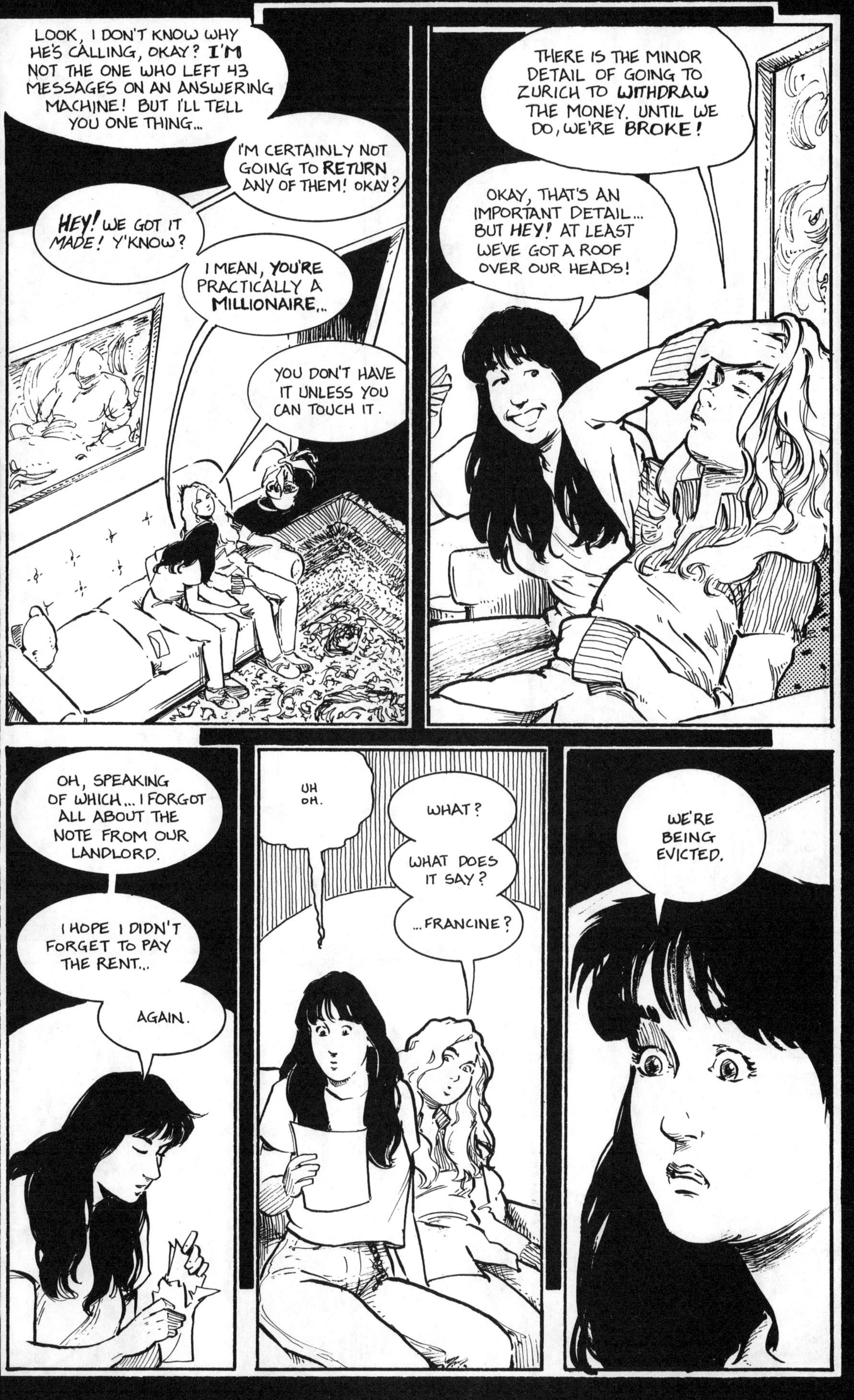
LOOK, I DON'T KNOW WHY HE'S CALLING, OKAY? I'M NOT THE ONE WHO LEFT 43 MESSAGES ON AN ANSWERING MACHINE! BUT I'LL TELL YOU ONE THING...
I'M CERTAINLY NOT GOING TO RETURN ANY OF THEM! OKAY?
HEY! WE GOT IT MADE! Y'KNOW?
I MEAN, YOU'RE PRACTICALLY A MILLIONAIRE...
YOU DON'T HAVE IT UNLESS YOU CAN TOUCH IT.
THERE IS THE MINOR DETAIL OF GOING TO ZURICH TO WITHDRAW THE MONEY. UNTIL WE DO, WE'RE BROKE!
OKAY, THAT'S AN IMPORTANT DETAIL... BUT HEY! AT LEAST WE'VE GOT A ROOF OVER OUR HEADS!
OH, SPEAKING OF WHICH... I FORGOT ALL ABOUT THE NOTE FROM OUR LANDLORD.
I HOPE I DIDN'T FORGET TO PAY THE RENT...
AGAIN.
UH OH.
WHAT?
WHAT DOES IT SAY?
...FRANCINE?
WE'RE BEING EVICTED.

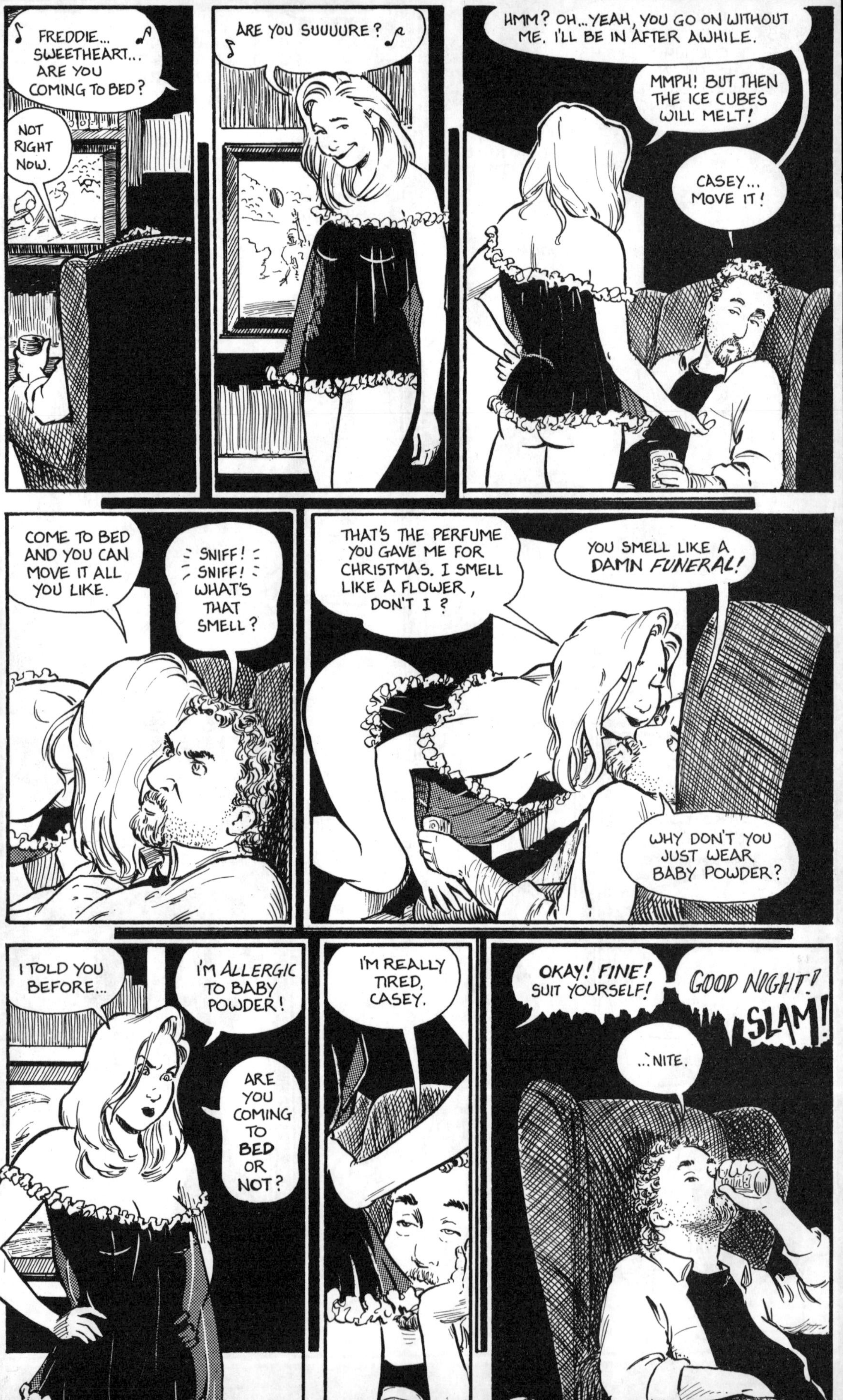
FREDDIE... SWEETHEART... ARE YOU COMING TO BED?
NOT RIGHT NOW.
ARE YOU SUUUURE?
HMM? OH...YEAH, YOU GO ON WITHOUT ME. I'LL BE IN AFTER AWHILE.
MMPH! BUT THEN THE ICE CUBES WILL MELT!
CASEY... MOVE IT!
COME TO BED AND YOU CAN MOVE IT ALL YOU LIKE.
SNIFF! SNIFF! WHAT'S THAT SMELL?
THAT'S THE PERFUME YOU GAVE ME FOR CHRISTMAS. I SMELL LIKE A FLOWER, DON'T I?
YOU SMELL LIKE A DAMN FUNERAL!
WHY DON'T YOU JUST WEAR BABY POWDER?
I TOLD YOU BEFORE...
I'M ALLERGIC TO BABY POWDER!
ARE YOU COMING TO BED OR NOT?
I'M REALLY TIRED, CASEY.
OKAY! FINE! SUIT YOURSELF!
GOOD NIGHT!
SLAM!
...NITE.

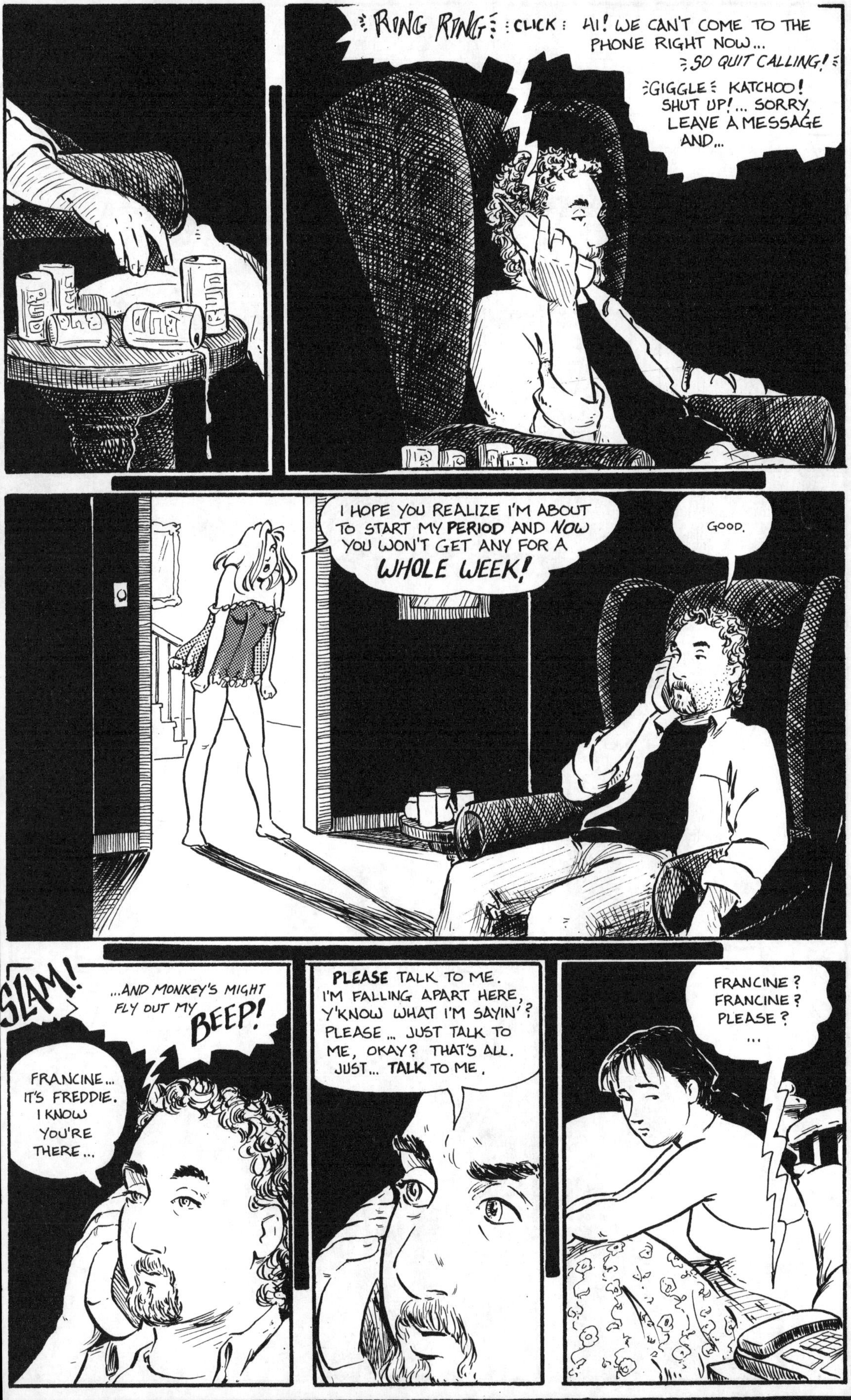

RING RING
CLICK
HI! WE CAN'T COME TO THE PHONE RIGHT NOW...
SO QUIT CALLING!
GIGGLE KATCHOO! SHUT UP!... SORRY, LEAVE A MESSAGE AND...
I HOPE YOU REALIZE I'M ABOUT TO START MY PERIOD AND NOW YOU WON'T GET ANY FOR A WHOLE WEEK!
GOOD.
SLAM!
...AND MONKEY'S MIGHT FLY OUT MY BEEP!
FRANCINE... IT'S FREDDIE. I KNOW YOU'RE THERE...
PLEASE TALK TO ME. I'M FALLING APART HERE, Y'KNOW WHAT I'M SAYIN'? PLEASE... JUST TALK TO ME, OKAY? THAT'S ALL. JUST... TALK TO ME.
FRANCINE? FRANCINE? PLEASE? ...

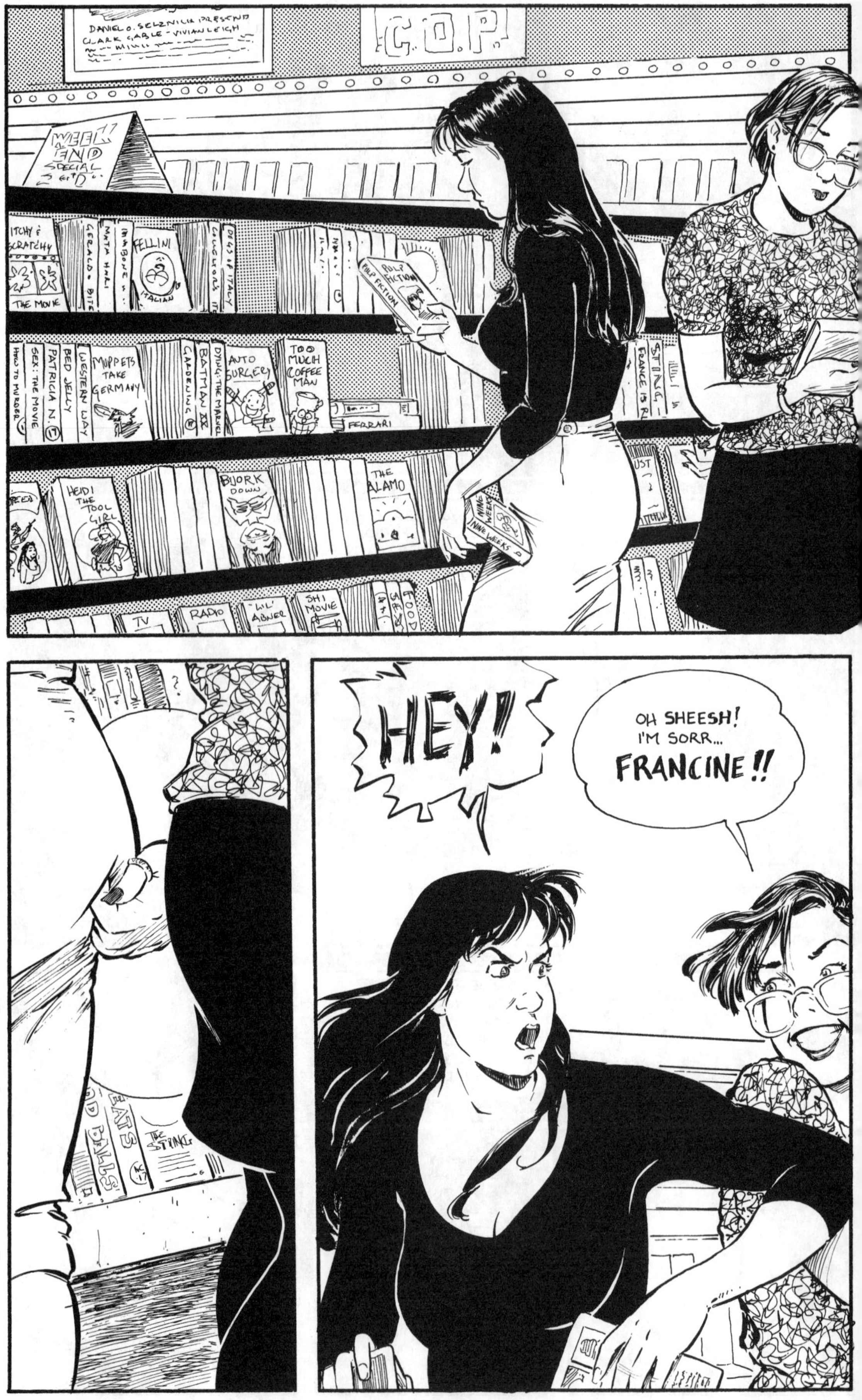
C.O.P.
DANIEL O. SELZNICK PRESENTS
CLARK GABLE - VIVIAN LEIGH
WEEK END SPECIAL
ITCHY & SCRATCHY THE MOVIE
MATA HARI
FELLINI
ITALIAN
DOGS OF ITALY
PULP FICTION
HOW TO MURDER
SEX: THE MOVIE
PATRICIA N.
BED JELLY
WESTERN WAY
MUPPETS TAKE GERMANY
GARDENING
BATMAN XX
DYING: THE MARVEL
AUTO SURGERY
TOO MUCH COFFEE MAN
FERRARI
HEIDI THE TOOL GIRL
BJORK DOWN
THE ALAMO
NINE WEEKS
TV
RADIO
"LIL' ABNER"
SHI MOVIE
THE STRING
HEY!
OH SHEESH!
I'M SORR...
FRANCINE!!

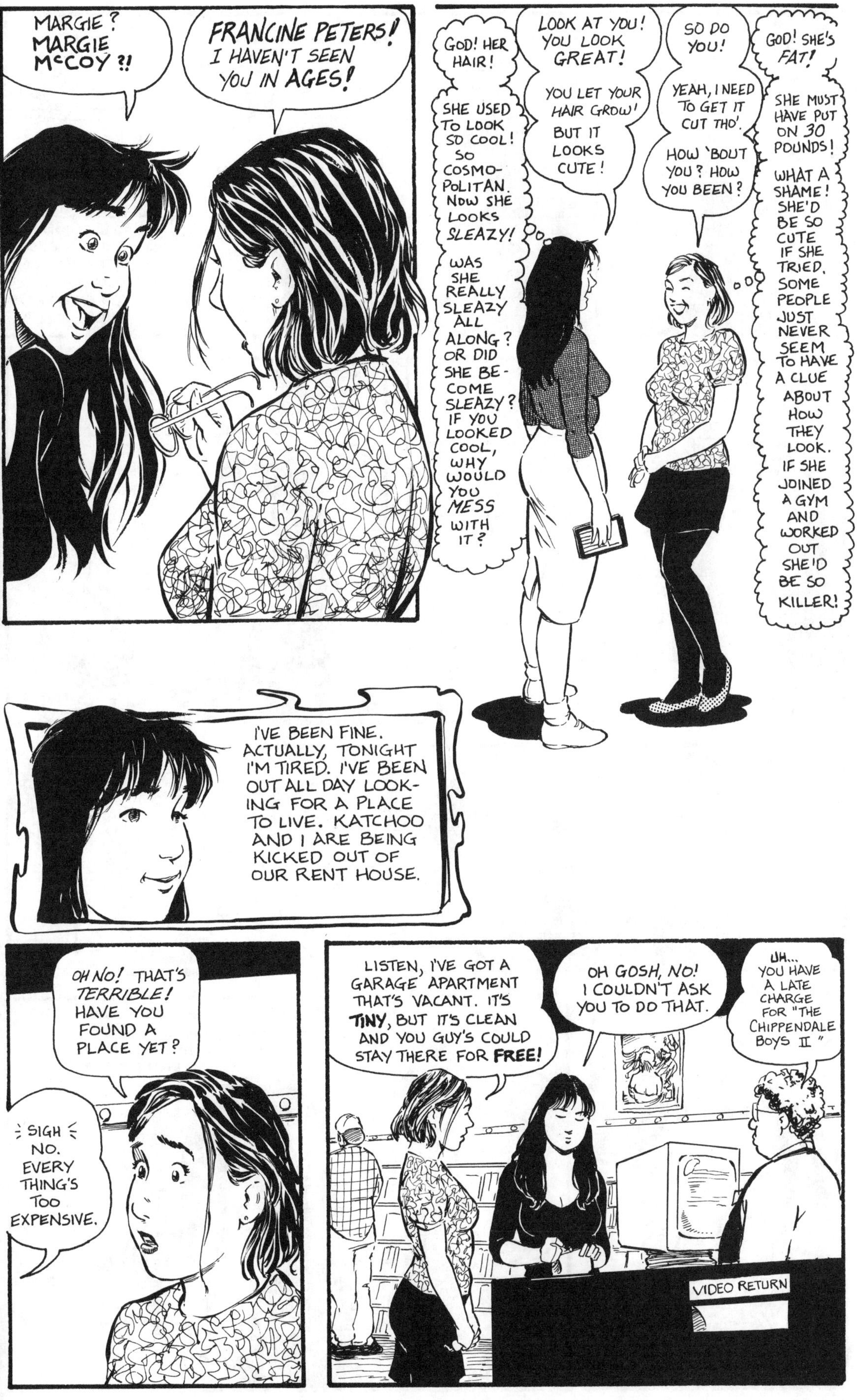
MARGIE? MARGIE McCOY?!
FRANCINE PETERS! I HAVEN'T SEEN YOU IN AGES!
GOD! HER HAIR!
SHE USED TO LOOK SO COOL! SO COSMO-POLITAN. NOW SHE LOOKS SLEAZY!
WAS SHE REALLY SLEAZY ALL ALONG? OR DID SHE BE-COME SLEAZY? IF YOU LOOKED COOL, WHY WOULD YOU MESS WITH IT?
LOOK AT YOU! YOU LOOK GREAT!
YOU LET YOUR HAIR GROW!
BUT IT LOOKS CUTE!
SO DO YOU!
YEAH, I NEED TO GET IT CUT THO'.
HOW 'BOUT YOU? HOW YOU BEEN?
GOD! SHE'S FAT!
SHE MUST HAVE PUT ON 30 POUNDS!
WHAT A SHAME! SHE'D BE SO CUTE IF SHE TRIED. SOME PEOPLE JUST NEVER SEEM TO HAVE A CLUE ABOUT HOW THEY LOOK. IF SHE JOINED A GYM AND WORKED OUT SHE'D BE SO KILLER!
I'VE BEEN FINE. ACTUALLY, TONIGHT I'M TIRED. I'VE BEEN OUT ALL DAY LOOK-ING FOR A PLACE TO LIVE. KATCHOO AND I ARE BEING KICKED OUT OF OUR RENT HOUSE.
OH NO! THAT'S TERRIBLE! HAVE YOU FOUND A PLACE YET?
SIGH NO. EVERY THING'S TOO EXPENSIVE.
LISTEN, I'VE GOT A GARAGE APARTMENT THAT'S VACANT. IT'S TINY, BUT IT'S CLEAN AND YOU GUY'S COULD STAY THERE FOR FREE!
OH GOSH, NO! I COULDN'T ASK YOU TO DO THAT.
UH... YOU HAVE A LATE CHARGE FOR "THE CHIPPENDALE BOYS II"
VIDEO RETURN

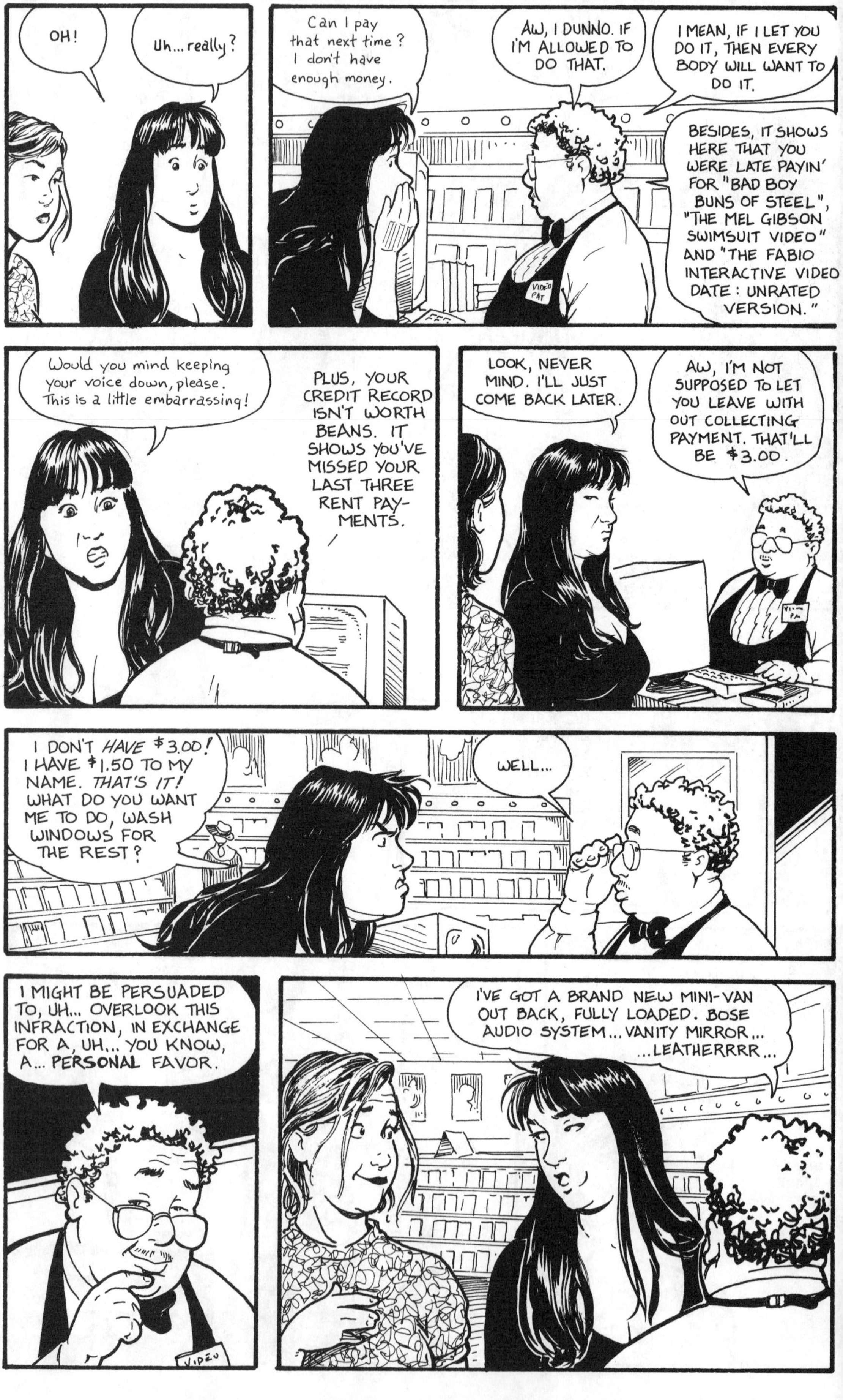
OH!
Uh... really?
Can I pay that next time? I don't have enough money.
AW, I DUNNO. IF I'M ALLOWED TO DO THAT.
I MEAN, IF I LET YOU DO IT, THEN EVERY BODY WILL WANT TO DO IT.
BESIDES, IT SHOWS HERE THAT YOU WERE LATE PAYIN' FOR "BAD BOY BUNS OF STEEL", "THE MEL GIBSON SWIMSUIT VIDEO" AND "THE FABIO INTERACTIVE VIDEO DATE: UNRATED VERSION."
VIDEO PAT
Would you mind keeping your voice down, please. This is a little embarrassing!
PLUS, YOUR CREDIT RECORD ISN'T WORTH BEANS. IT SHOWS YOU'VE MISSED YOUR LAST THREE RENT PAY-MENTS.
LOOK, NEVER MIND. I'LL JUST COME BACK LATER.
AW, I'M NOT SUPPOSED TO LET YOU LEAVE WITH OUT COLLECTING PAYMENT. THAT'LL BE $3.00.
I DON'T *HAVE* $3.00! I HAVE $1.50 TO MY NAME. *THAT'S IT!* WHAT DO YOU WANT ME TO DO, WASH WINDOWS FOR THE REST?
WELL...
I MIGHT BE PERSUADED TO, UH... OVERLOOK THIS INFRACTION, IN EXCHANGE FOR A, UH... YOU KNOW, A... **PERSONAL** FAVOR.
VIDEO
I'VE GOT A BRAND NEW MINI-VAN OUT BACK, FULLY LOADED. BOSE AUDIO SYSTEM... VANITY MIRROR... ...LEATHERRRR...

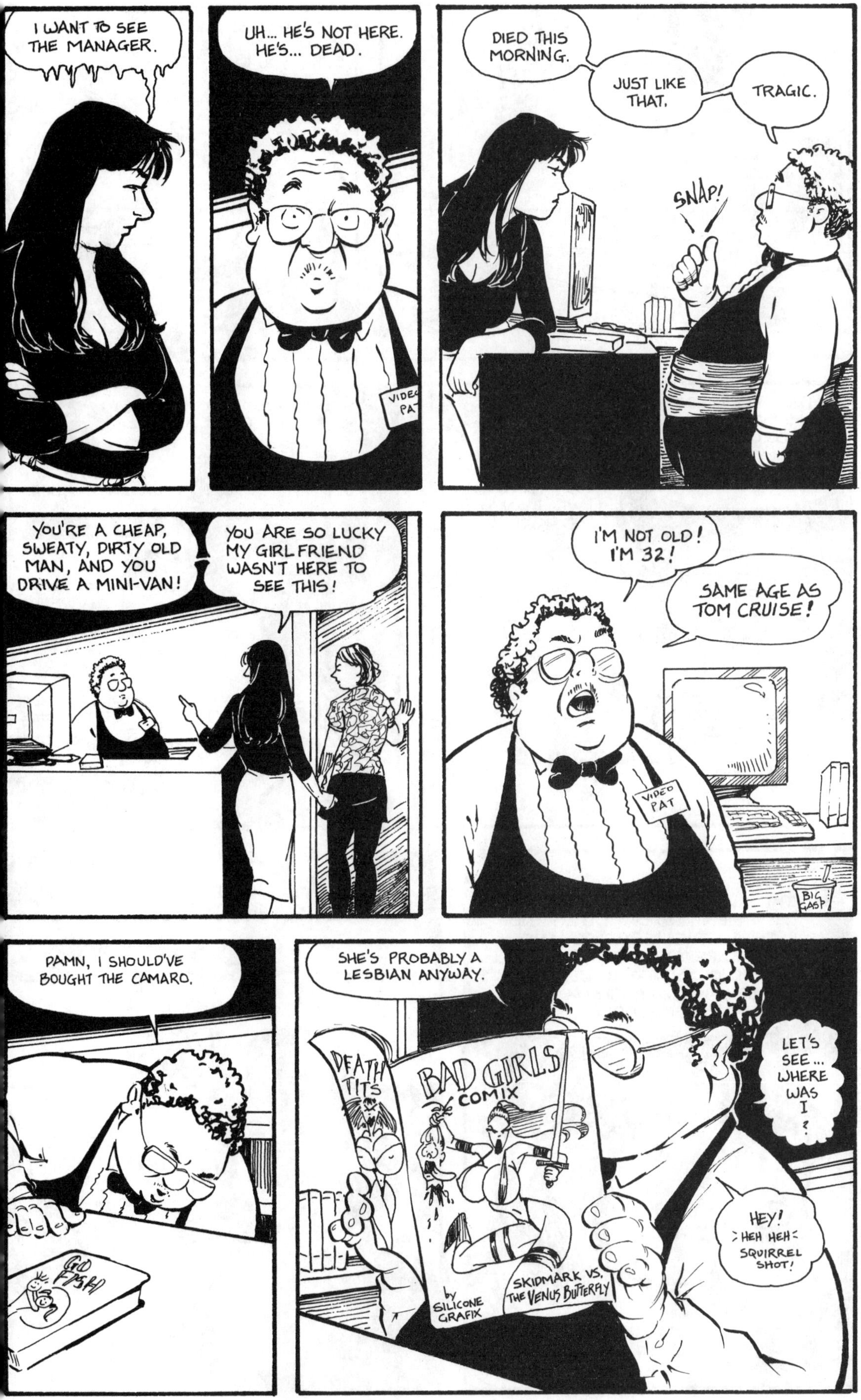
I WANT TO SEE THE MANAGER.
UH... HE'S NOT HERE. HE'S... DEAD.
VIDEO PAT
DIED THIS MORNING.
JUST LIKE THAT.
TRAGIC.
SNAP!
YOU'RE A CHEAP, SWEATY, DIRTY OLD MAN, AND YOU DRIVE A MINI-VAN!
YOU ARE SO LUCKY MY GIRL FRIEND WASN'T HERE TO SEE THIS!
I'M NOT OLD! I'M 32!
SAME AGE AS TOM CRUISE!
VIDEO PAT
BIG GASP
DAMN, I SHOULD'VE BOUGHT THE CAMARO.
GO FISH
SHE'S PROBABLY A LESBIAN ANYWAY.
LET'S SEE... WHERE WAS I?
DEATH TITS
BAD GIRLS COMIX
SKIDMARK VS. THE VENUS BUTTERFLY
by SILICONE GRAFIX
HEY! HEH HEH SQUIRREL SHOT!

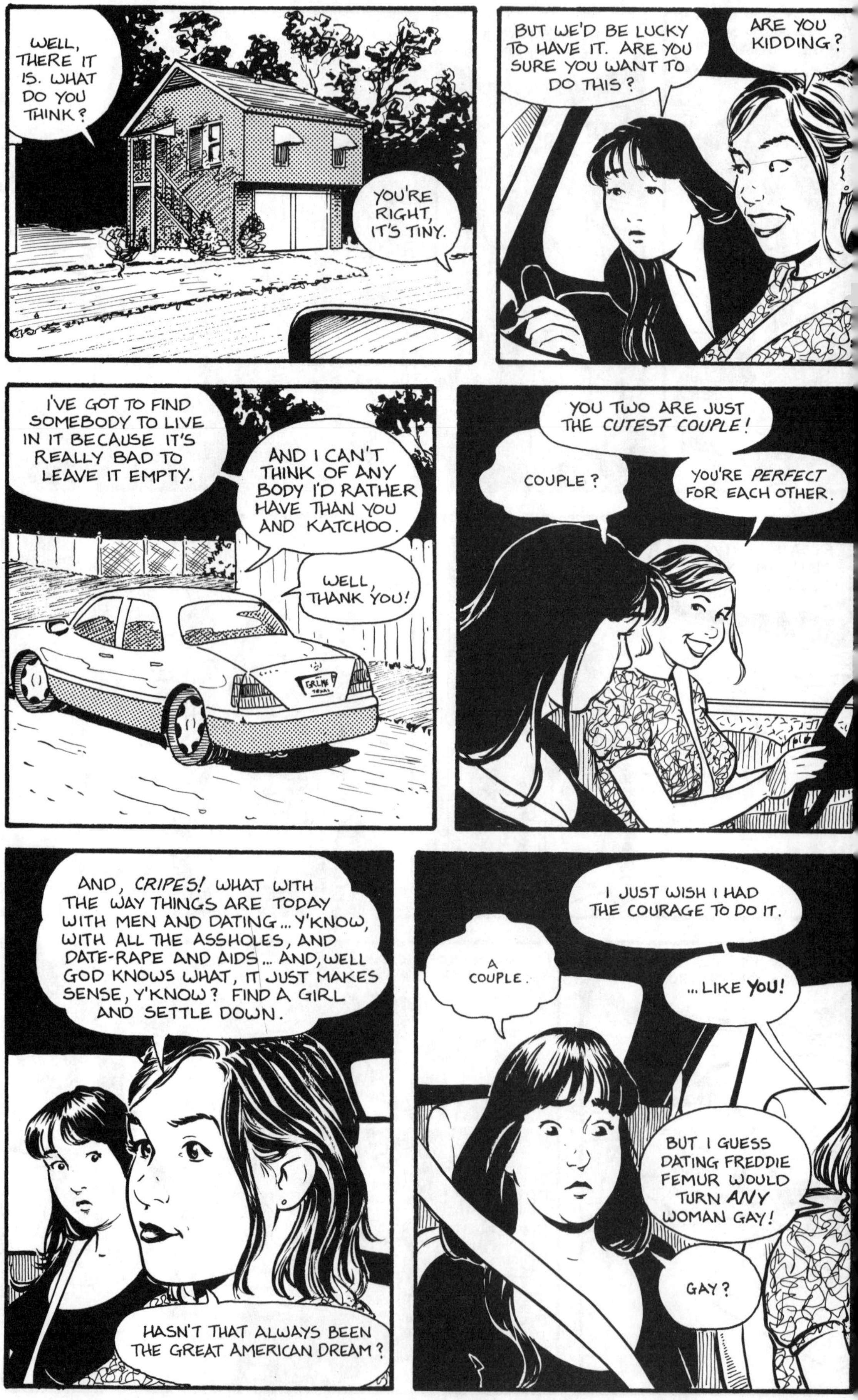
WELL, THERE IT IS. WHAT DO YOU THINK?
YOU'RE RIGHT, IT'S TINY.
BUT WE'D BE LUCKY TO HAVE IT. ARE YOU SURE YOU WANT TO DO THIS?
ARE YOU KIDDING?
I'VE GOT TO FIND SOMEBODY TO LIVE IN IT BECAUSE IT'S REALLY BAD TO LEAVE IT EMPTY.
AND I CAN'T THINK OF ANY BODY I'D RATHER HAVE THAN YOU AND KATCHOO.
WELL, THANK YOU!
YOU TWO ARE JUST THE *CUTEST COUPLE*!
COUPLE?
YOU'RE *PERFECT* FOR EACH OTHER.
AND, *CRIPES!* WHAT WITH THE WAY THINGS ARE TODAY WITH MEN AND DATING... Y'KNOW, WITH ALL THE ASSHOLES, AND DATE-RAPE AND AIDS... AND, WELL GOD KNOWS WHAT, IT JUST MAKES SENSE, Y'KNOW? FIND A GIRL AND SETTLE DOWN.
HASN'T THAT ALWAYS BEEN THE GREAT AMERICAN DREAM?
I JUST WISH I HAD THE COURAGE TO DO IT.
A COUPLE.
...LIKE **YOU**!
BUT I GUESS DATING FREDDIE FEMUR WOULD TURN *ANY* WOMAN GAY!
GAY?

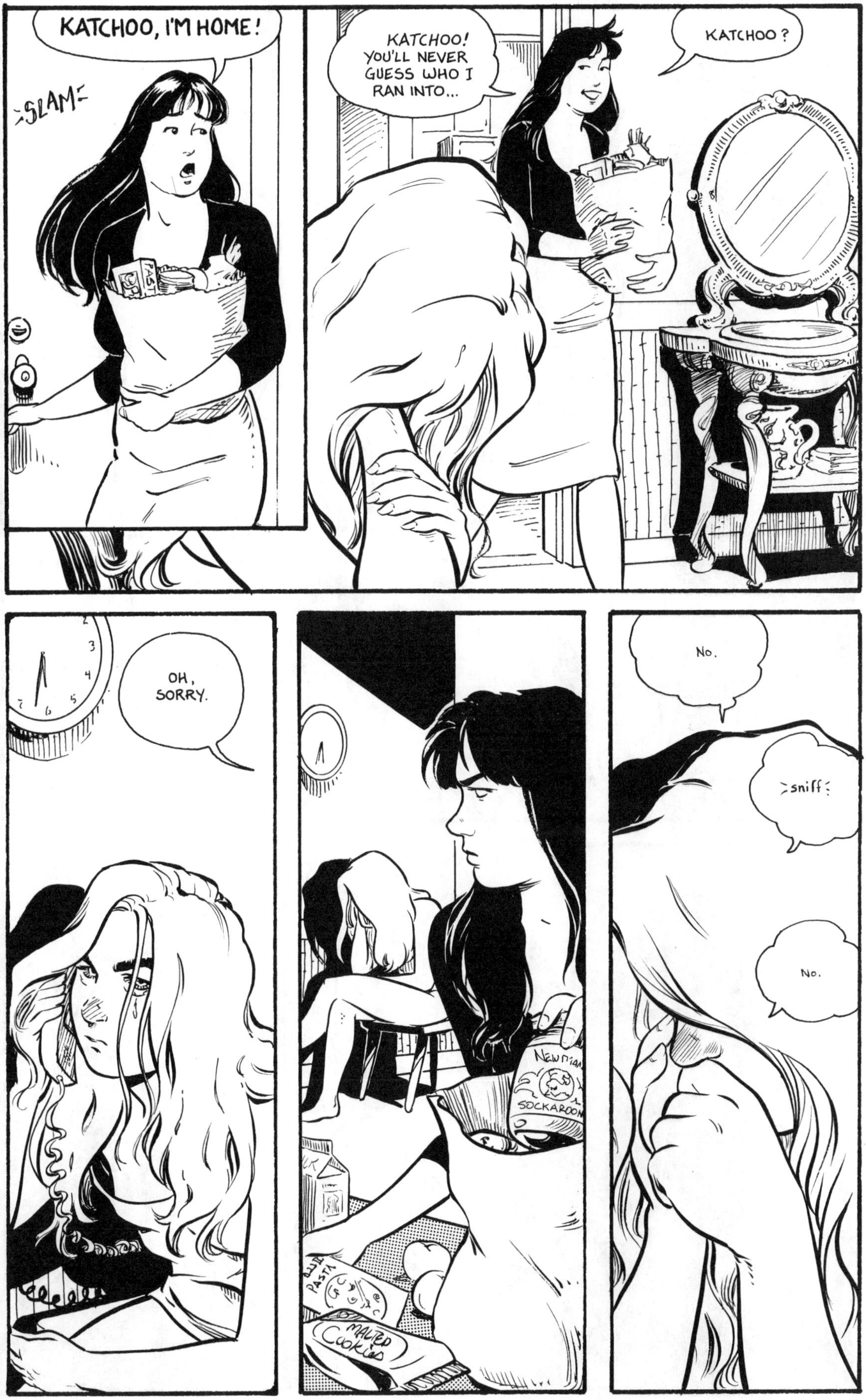
KATCHOO, I'M HOME!
SLAM
KATCHOO! YOU'LL NEVER GUESS WHO I RAN INTO...
KATCHOO?
OH, SORRY.
No.
sniff
No.
SOCKAROONI
PASTA
MALTED Cookies

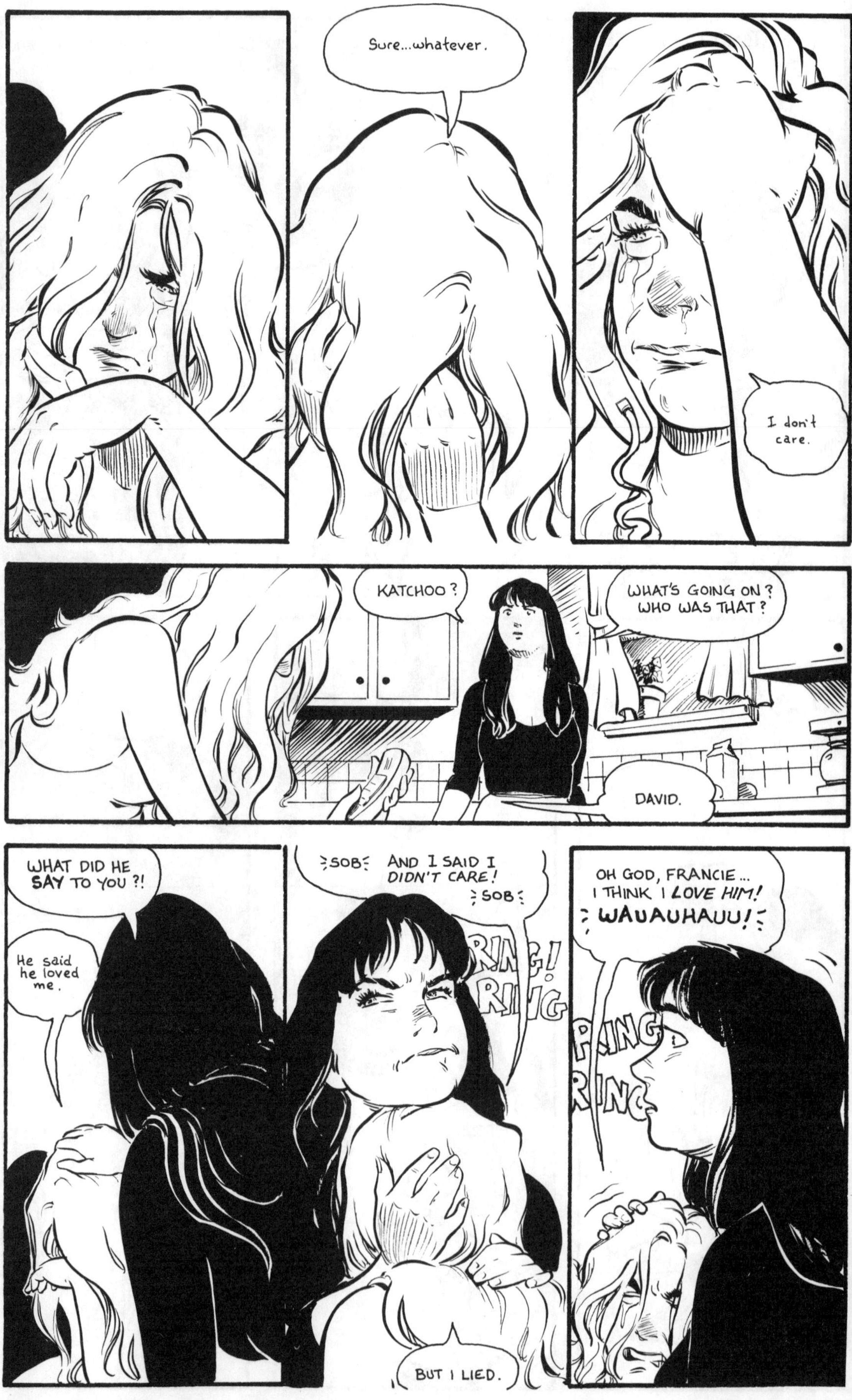
Sure...whatever.
I don't care.
KATCHOO?
WHAT'S GOING ON? WHO WAS THAT?
DAVID.
WHAT DID HE SAY TO YOU ?!
He said he loved me.
SOB AND I SAID I DIDN'T CARE! SOB
BUT I LIED.
OH GOD, FRANCIE... I THINK I LOVE HIM! WAUAUHAUU!

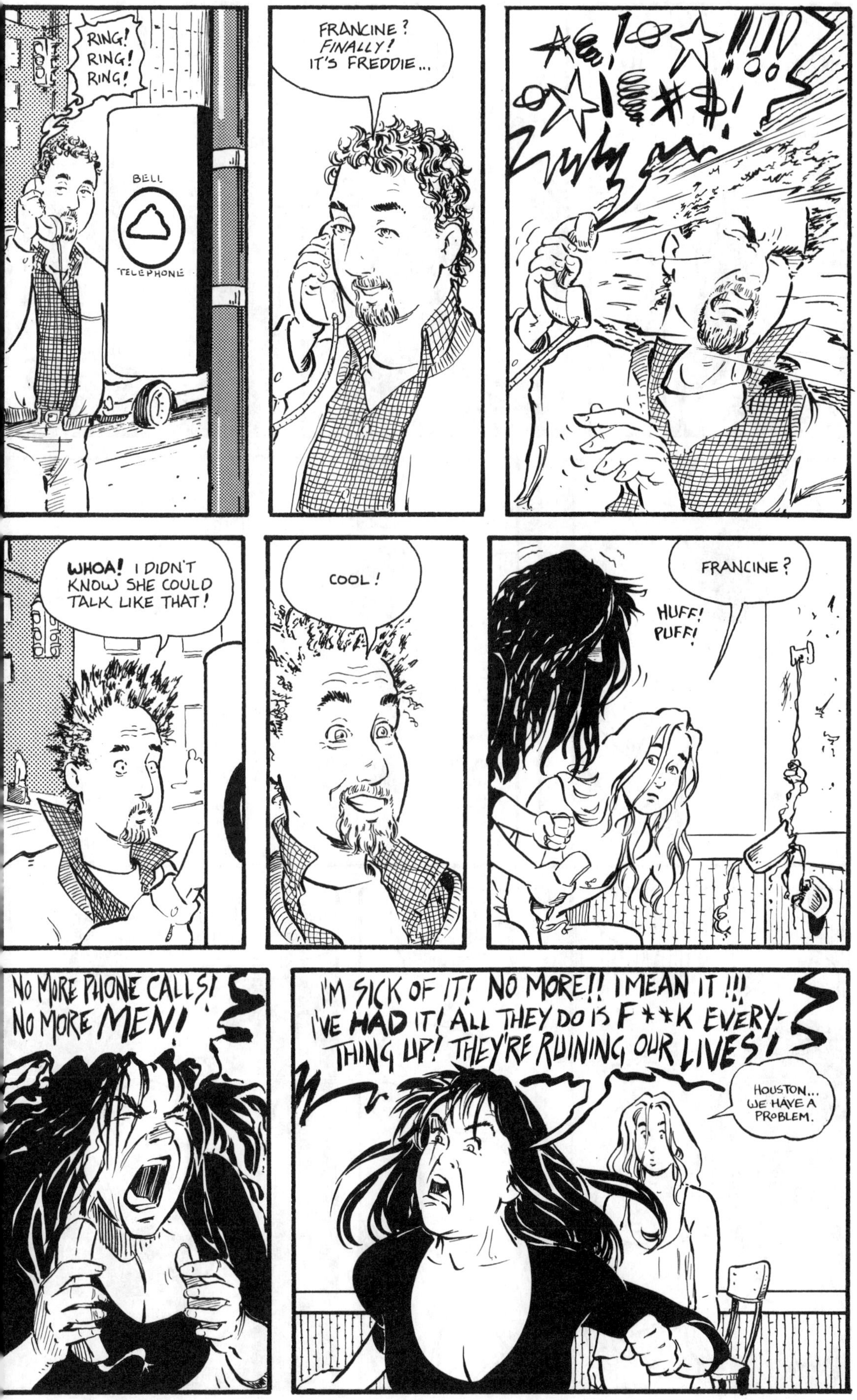
RING! RING! RING!
BELL
TELEPHONE
FRANCINE? FINALLY! IT'S FREDDIE...
WHOA! I DIDN'T KNOW SHE COULD TALK LIKE THAT!
COOL!
HUFF! PUFF!
FRANCINE?
NO MORE PHONE CALLS! NO MORE MEN!
I'M SICK OF IT! NO MORE!! I MEAN IT!!! I'VE HAD IT! ALL THEY DO IS F**K EVERY-THING UP! THEY'RE RUINING OUR LIVES!
HOUSTON... WE HAVE A PROBLEM.

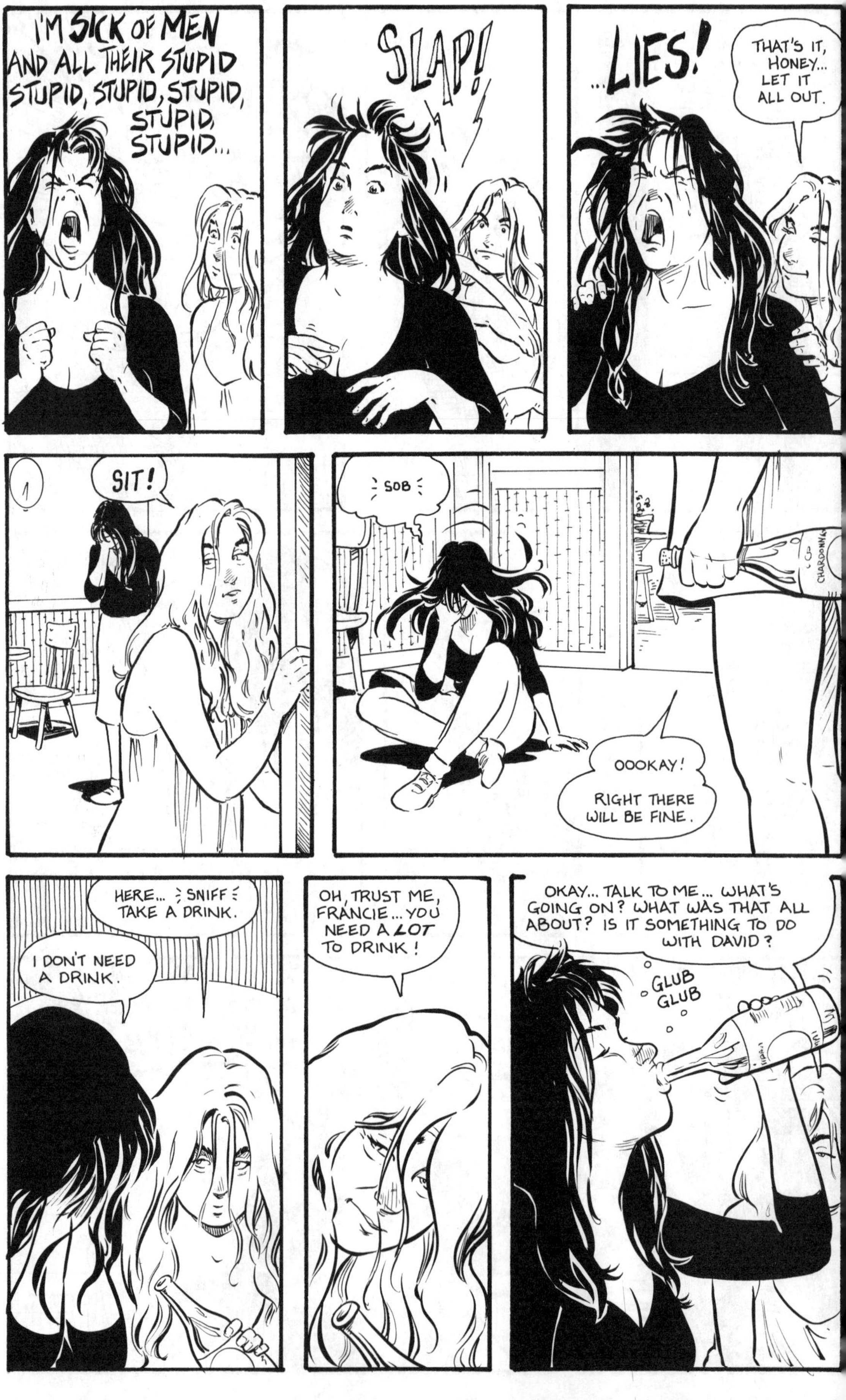
I'M SICK OF MEN AND ALL THEIR STUPID STUPID, STUPID, STUPID, STUPID, STUPID...
SLAP!
...LIES!
THAT'S IT, HONEY... LET IT ALL OUT.
SIT!
SOB
CHARDONNAY
OOOKAY!
RIGHT THERE WILL BE FINE.
HERE... SNIFF TAKE A DRINK.
I DON'T NEED A DRINK.
OH, TRUST ME, FRANCIE... YOU NEED A LOT TO DRINK!
OKAY... TALK TO ME... WHAT'S GOING ON? WHAT WAS THAT ALL ABOUT? IS IT SOMETHING TO DO WITH DAVID?
GLUB GLUB

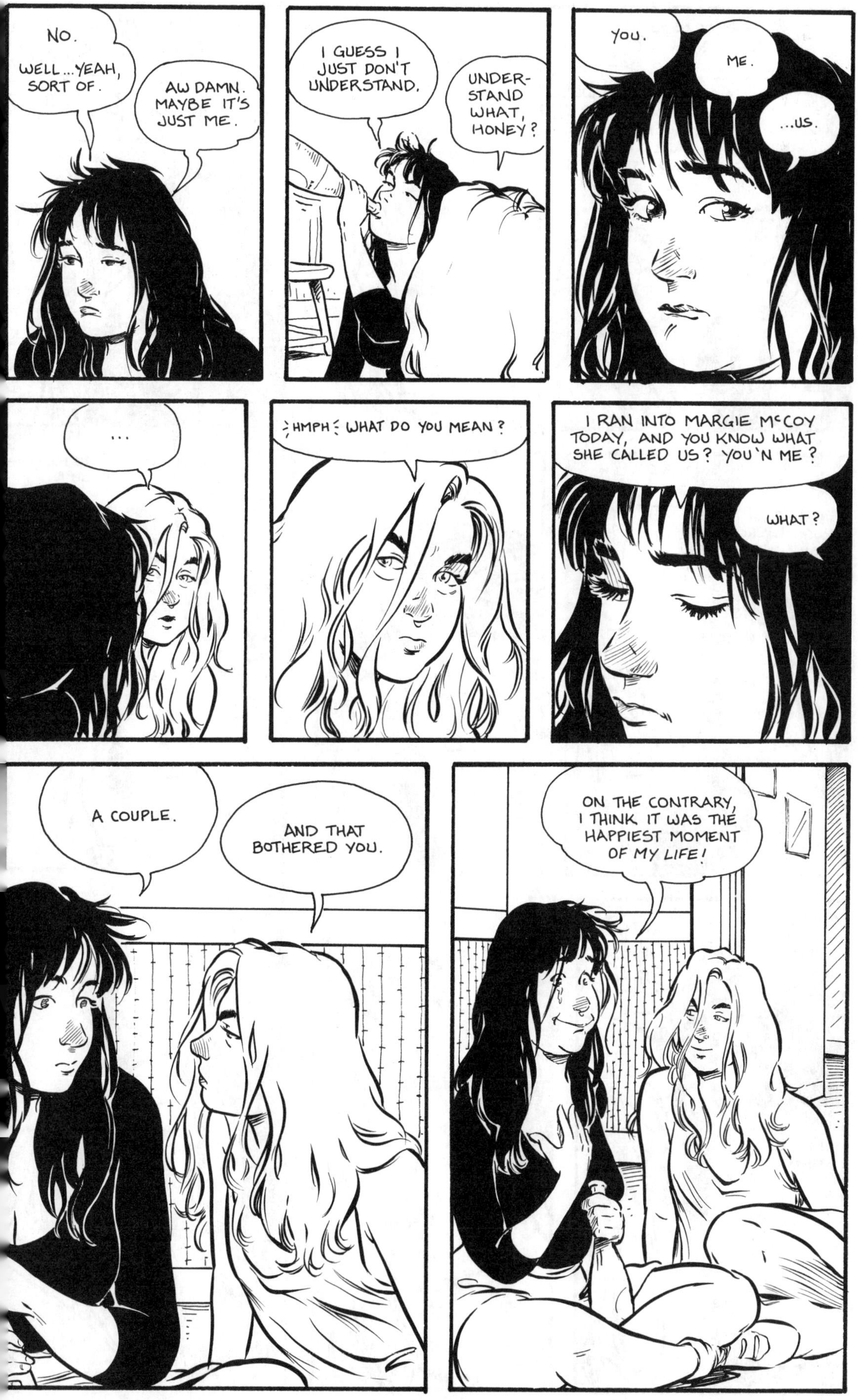
NO.
WELL... YEAH, SORT OF.
AW DAMN. MAYBE IT'S JUST ME.
I GUESS I JUST DON'T UNDERSTAND.
UNDER-STAND WHAT, HONEY?
YOU.
ME.
...US.
...
HMPH WHAT DO YOU MEAN?
I RAN INTO MARGIE McCOY TODAY, AND YOU KNOW WHAT SHE CALLED US? YOU'N ME?
WHAT?
A COUPLE.
AND THAT BOTHERED YOU.
ON THE CONTRARY, I THINK IT WAS THE HAPPIEST MOMENT OF MY LIFE!

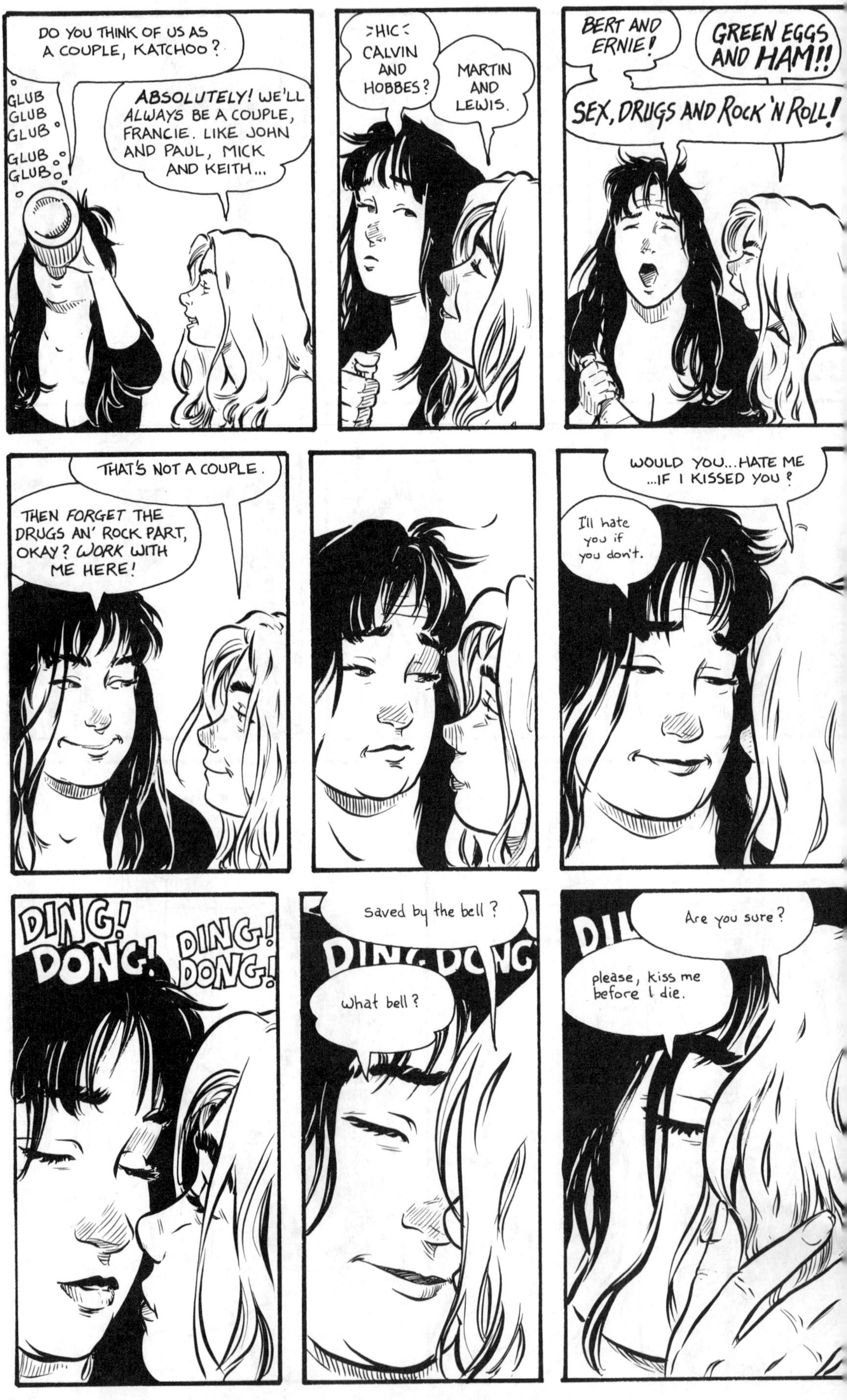
DO YOU THINK OF US AS A COUPLE, KATCHOO?
GLUB GLUB GLUB GLUB GLUB
ABSOLUTELY! WE'LL ALWAYS BE A COUPLE, FRANCIE. LIKE JOHN AND PAUL, MICK AND KEITH...
HIC CALVIN AND HOBBES?
MARTIN AND LEWIS.
BERT AND ERNIE!
GREEN EGGS AND HAM!!
SEX, DRUGS AND ROCK 'N ROLL!
THAT'S NOT A COUPLE.
THEN FORGET THE DRUGS AN' ROCK PART, OKAY? WORK WITH ME HERE!
WOULD YOU...HATE ME ...IF I KISSED YOU?
I'll hate you if you don't.
DING! DONG! DING! DONG!
saved by the bell?
DING DONG
what bell?
Are you sure?
please, kiss me before I die.

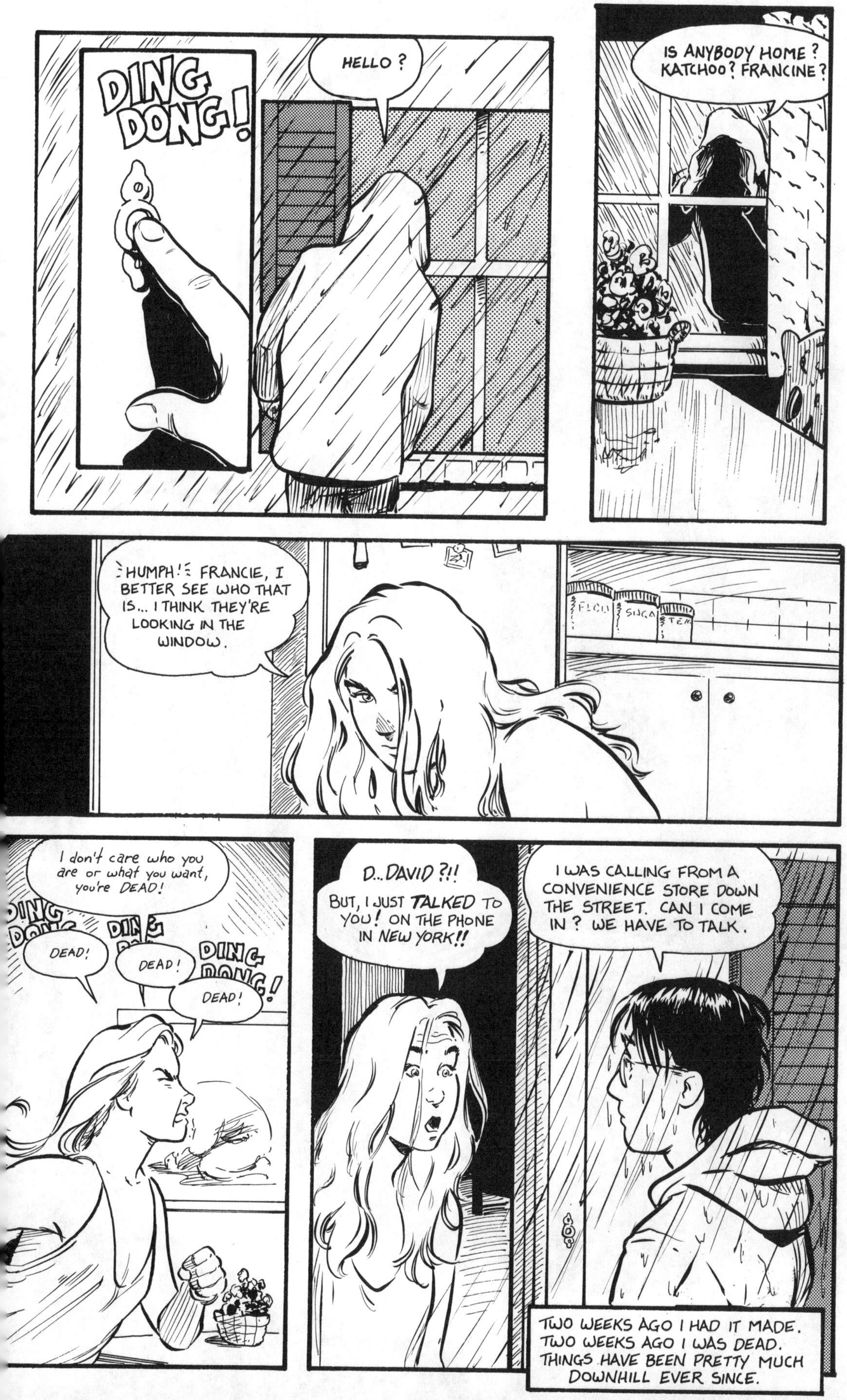
DING DONG!
HELLO ?
IS ANYBODY HOME ? KATCHOO? FRANCINE ?
HUMPH! FRANCIE, I BETTER SEE WHO THAT IS... I THINK THEY'RE LOOKING IN THE WINDOW.
FLOU
SUGA
TEA
I don't care who you are or what you want, you're DEAD!
DEAD!
DEAD!
DING DONG!
DEAD!
D...DAVID ?!!
BUT, I JUST TALKED TO YOU! ON THE PHONE IN NEW YORK!!
I WAS CALLING FROM A CONVENIENCE STORE DOWN THE STREET. CAN I COME IN ? WE HAVE TO TALK.
TWO WEEKS AGO I HAD IT MADE. TWO WEEKS AGO I WAS DEAD. THINGS HAVE BEEN PRETTY MUCH DOWNHILL EVER SINCE.

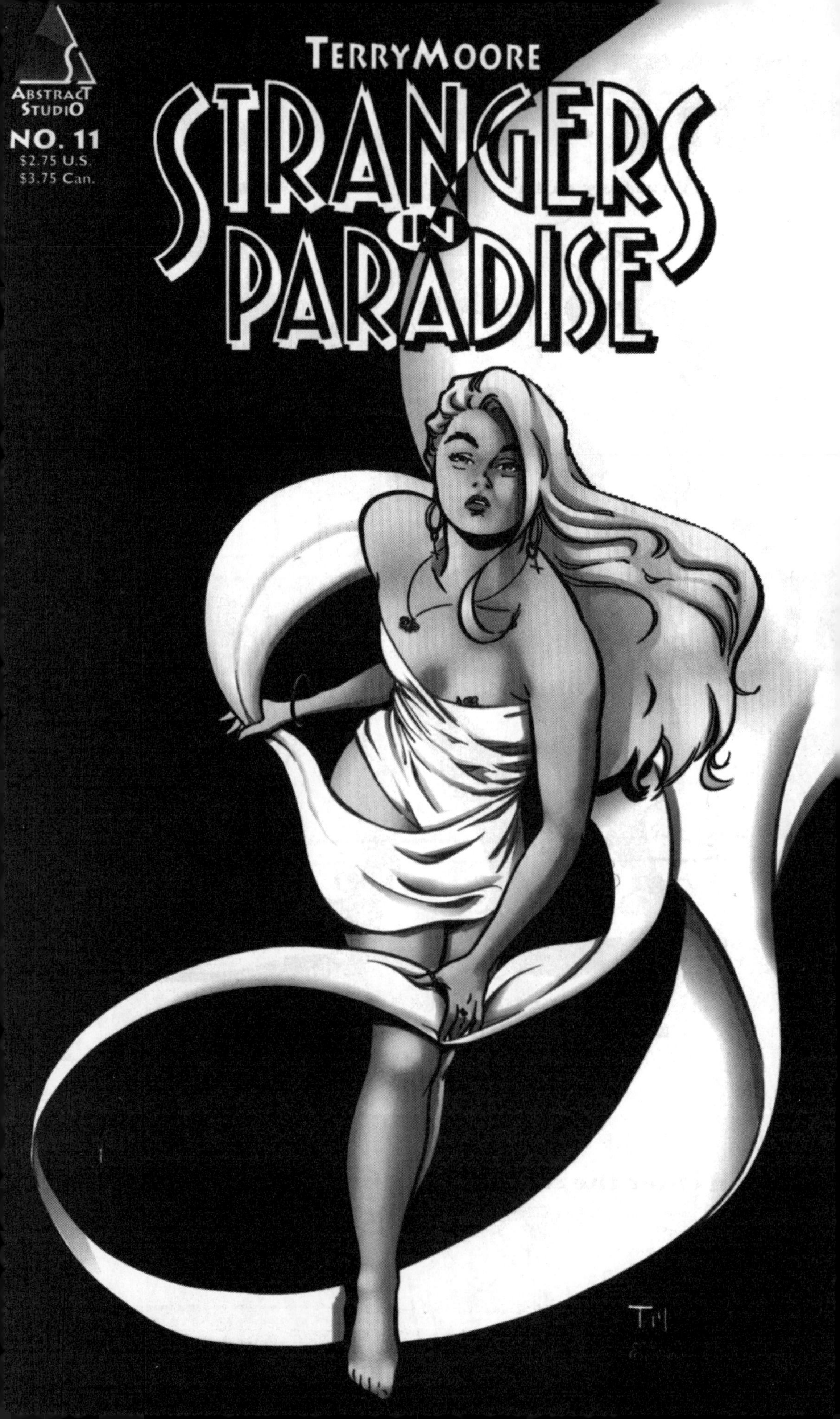

Abstract Studio
NO. 11
$2.75 U.S.
$3.75 Can.
Terry Moore
Strangers in Paradise

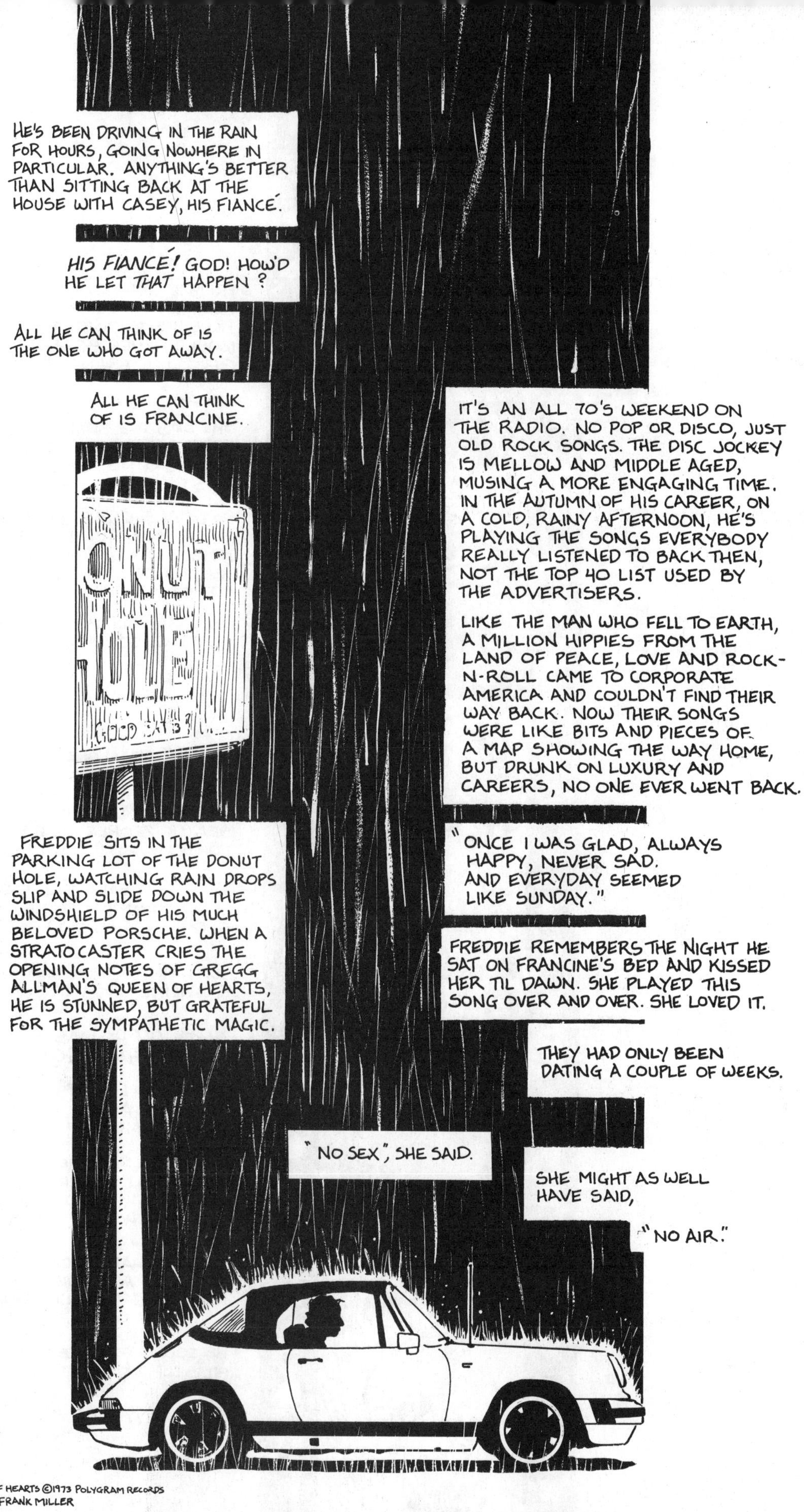
HE'S BEEN DRIVING IN THE RAIN FOR HOURS, GOING NOWHERE IN PARTICULAR. ANYTHING'S BETTER THAN SITTING BACK AT THE HOUSE WITH CASEY, HIS FIANCÉ.
HIS FIANCÉ! GOD! HOW'D HE LET THAT HAPPEN ?
ALL HE CAN THINK OF IS THE ONE WHO GOT AWAY.
ALL HE CAN THINK OF IS FRANCINE.
IT'S AN ALL 70'S WEEKEND ON THE RADIO. NO POP OR DISCO, JUST OLD ROCK SONGS. THE DISC JOCKEY IS MELLOW AND MIDDLE AGED, MUSING A MORE ENGAGING TIME. IN THE AUTUMN OF HIS CAREER, ON A COLD, RAINY AFTERNOON, HE'S PLAYING THE SONGS EVERYBODY REALLY LISTENED TO BACK THEN, NOT THE TOP 40 LIST USED BY THE ADVERTISERS.
LIKE THE MAN WHO FELL TO EARTH, A MILLION HIPPIES FROM THE LAND OF PEACE, LOVE AND ROCK-N-ROLL CAME TO CORPORATE AMERICA AND COULDN'T FIND THEIR WAY BACK. NOW THEIR SONGS WERE LIKE BITS AND PIECES OF A MAP SHOWING THE WAY HOME, BUT DRUNK ON LUXURY AND CAREERS, NO ONE EVER WENT BACK.
FREDDIE SITS IN THE PARKING LOT OF THE DONUT HOLE, WATCHING RAIN DROPS SLIP AND SLIDE DOWN THE WINDSHIELD OF HIS MUCH BELOVED PORSCHE. WHEN A STRATOCASTER CRIES THE OPENING NOTES OF GREGG ALLMAN'S QUEEN OF HEARTS, HE IS STUNNED, BUT GRATEFUL FOR THE SYMPATHETIC MAGIC.
"ONCE I WAS GLAD, ALWAYS HAPPY, NEVER SAD. AND EVERYDAY SEEMED LIKE SUNDAY."
FREDDIE REMEMBERS THE NIGHT HE SAT ON FRANCINE'S BED AND KISSED HER TIL DAWN. SHE PLAYED THIS SONG OVER AND OVER. SHE LOVED IT.
THEY HAD ONLY BEEN DATING A COUPLE OF WEEKS.
"NO SEX", SHE SAID.
SHE MIGHT AS WELL HAVE SAID,
"NO AIR."

"AND AFTER ALL THAT
   WE'VE BEEN THROUGH,
   I FIND THAT WHEN I
   THINK OF YOU,
   A WARM SOUTH WIND
   RUNS THROUGH
   AND THROUGH.
   AND IN MY HEART
   THERE'S ONLY YOU."

"AND I WILL ALWAYS KEEP
   ON TRYIN'
   TO GATHER THIS STRANGE
   PEACE OF MIND.
   WITHOUT IT THERE'D BE
   LONELY ME,
   AND, OH DARLING,
   LONELY YOU."

"I LOVE YOU, QUEEN OF
   HEARTS.
   DON'T TELL ME WHEN
   TO STOP,
   TELL ME WHEN TO START."

FREDDIE PURSES HIS LIPS
AGAINST THE LUMP THAT
FILLS HIS THROAT. THERE
WOULD NEVER BE ANOTHER
GIRL LIKE FRANCINE.

NEVER.

SHE WAS THE SEXIEST,
MOST BEAUTIFUL, MOST
INTOXICATING, SEXIEST,
MOST... SEXY... SEX...

OH GOD! SHE WAS PERFECT!
EXCEPT FOR THAT LITTLE
TONGUE THINGY SHE DID TO
HER TEETH AFTER SHE ATE,
BUT OTHER THAN THAT...

OH, LORD HELP HIM, WHERE
DID IT ALL GO WRONG?

HEY! HE WAS LONELY! HE
WAS MORE LONELY THAN
HE'D BEEN HIS ENTIRE
LIFE. ALL ALONE IN A
SEA OF PEOPLE. IN HIS
PORSCHE. IN HIS OWN BED.

EVEN GOD SAID IT WASN'T
GOOD FOR MAN TO BE
ALONE, IN HIS OWN BED.

GOD WANTED HIM TO HAVE
FRANCINE, DAMMIT!

THAT'S IT! HE WAS ON A
MISSION FROM GOD!

HE HAD TO BE WITH
FRANCINE AGAIN. SHE
HAD TO TAKE HIM BACK!

HE SHOULD DO SOMETHING.
HE SHOULD GO OVER
THERE RIGHT NOW AND
TELL HER HOW HE FEELS.

THAT'S WHAT HE OUGHT
TO DO. THAT'S WHAT
A REAL MAN WOULD DO.

HE COULD PICTURE
HIMSELF DOING THAT.

WELL, HE COULD!

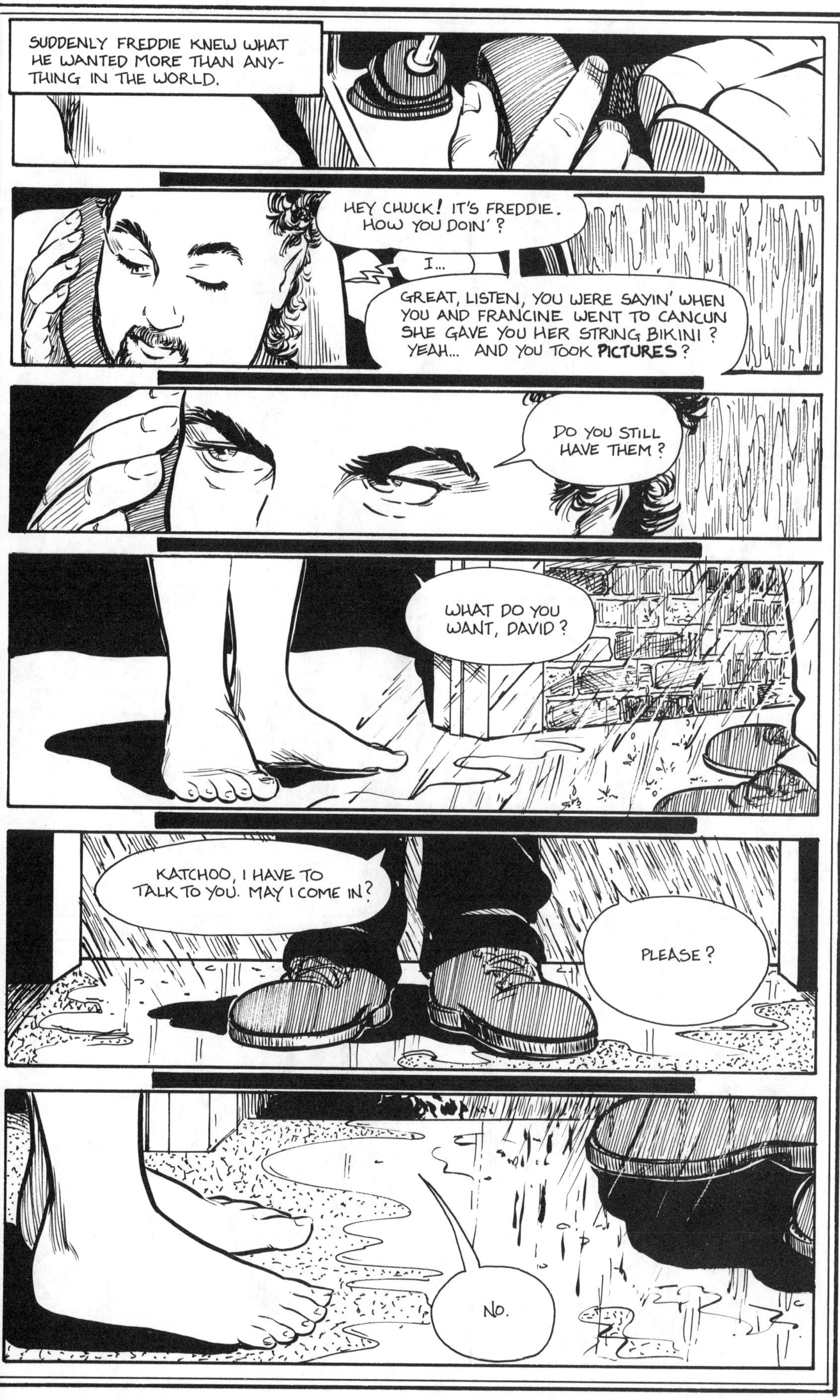
SUDDENLY FREDDIE KNEW WHAT HE WANTED MORE THAN ANY-THING IN THE WORLD.
HEY CHUCK! IT'S FREDDIE. HOW YOU DOIN'?
I...
GREAT, LISTEN, YOU WERE SAYIN' WHEN YOU AND FRANCINE WENT TO CANCUN SHE GAVE YOU HER STRING BIKINI? YEAH... AND YOU TOOK PICTURES?
DO YOU STILL HAVE THEM?
WHAT DO YOU WANT, DAVID?
KATCHOO, I HAVE TO TALK TO YOU. MAY I COME IN?
PLEASE?
NO.

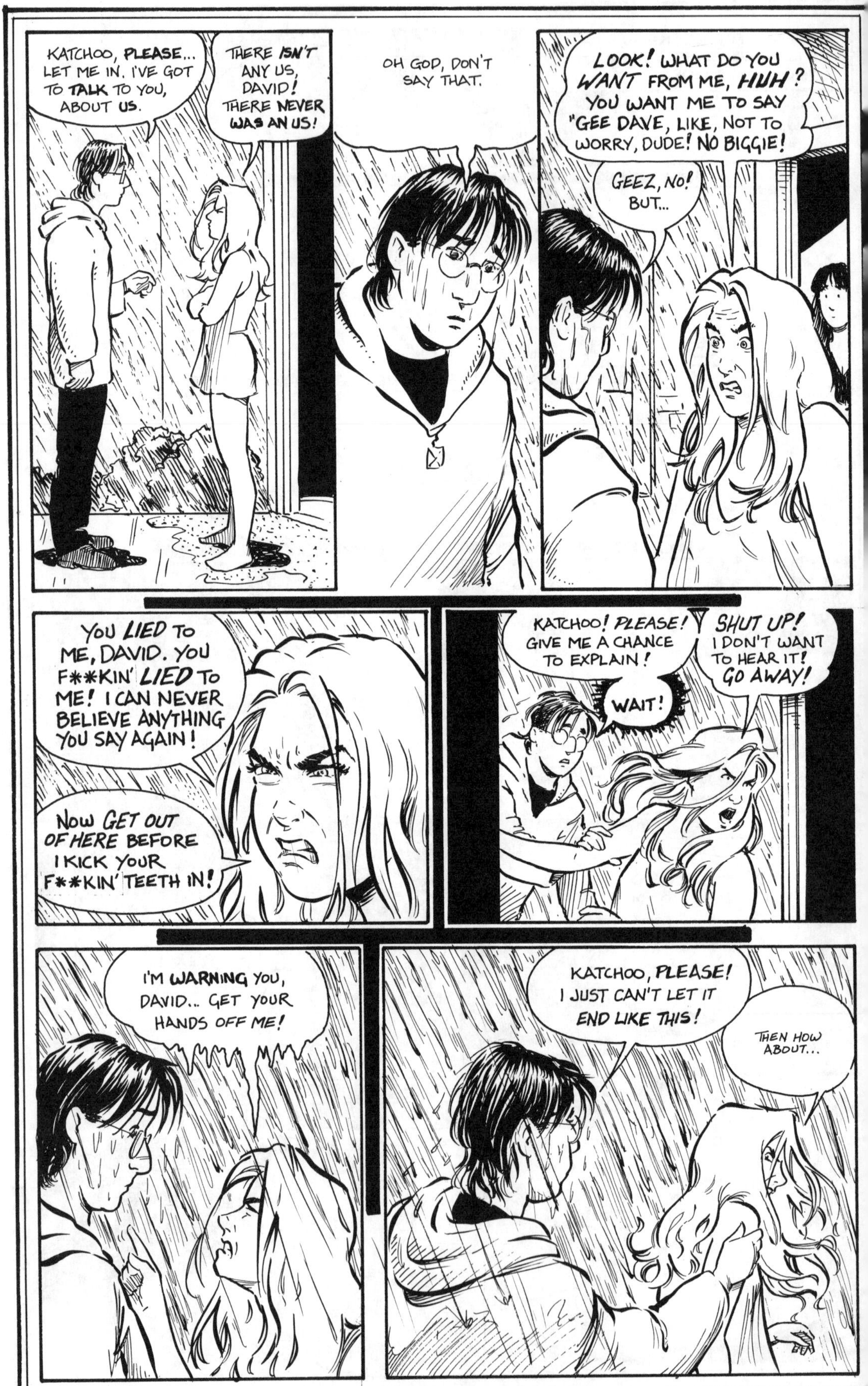
KATCHOO, PLEASE... LET ME IN. I'VE GOT TO TALK TO YOU, ABOUT US.
THERE ISN'T ANY US, DAVID! THERE NEVER WAS AN US!
OH GOD, DON'T SAY THAT.
LOOK! WHAT DO YOU WANT FROM ME, HUH? YOU WANT ME TO SAY "GEE DAVE, LIKE, NOT TO WORRY, DUDE! NO BIGGIE!
GEEZ, NO! BUT...
YOU LIED TO ME, DAVID. YOU F**KIN' LIED TO ME! I CAN NEVER BELIEVE ANYTHING YOU SAY AGAIN!
NOW GET OUT OF HERE BEFORE I KICK YOUR F**KIN' TEETH IN!
KATCHOO! PLEASE! GIVE ME A CHANCE TO EXPLAIN!
SHUT UP! I DON'T WANT TO HEAR IT! GO AWAY!
WAIT!
I'M WARNING YOU, DAVID... GET YOUR HANDS OFF ME!
KATCHOO, PLEASE! I JUST CAN'T LET IT END LIKE THIS!
THEN HOW ABOUT...

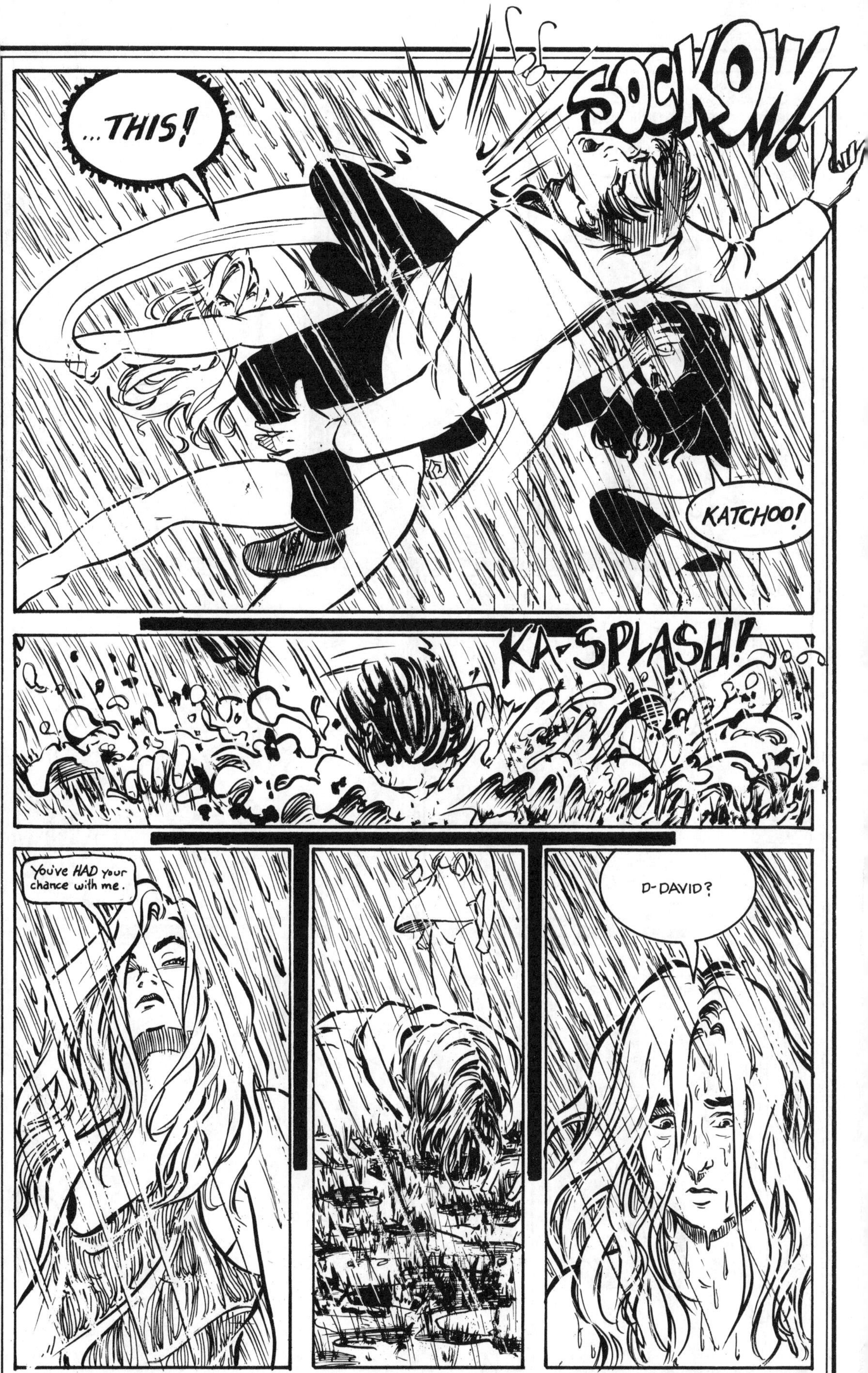
...THIS!
SOCKOW!
KATCHOO!
KA-SPLASH!
You've HAD your chance with me.
D-DAVID?

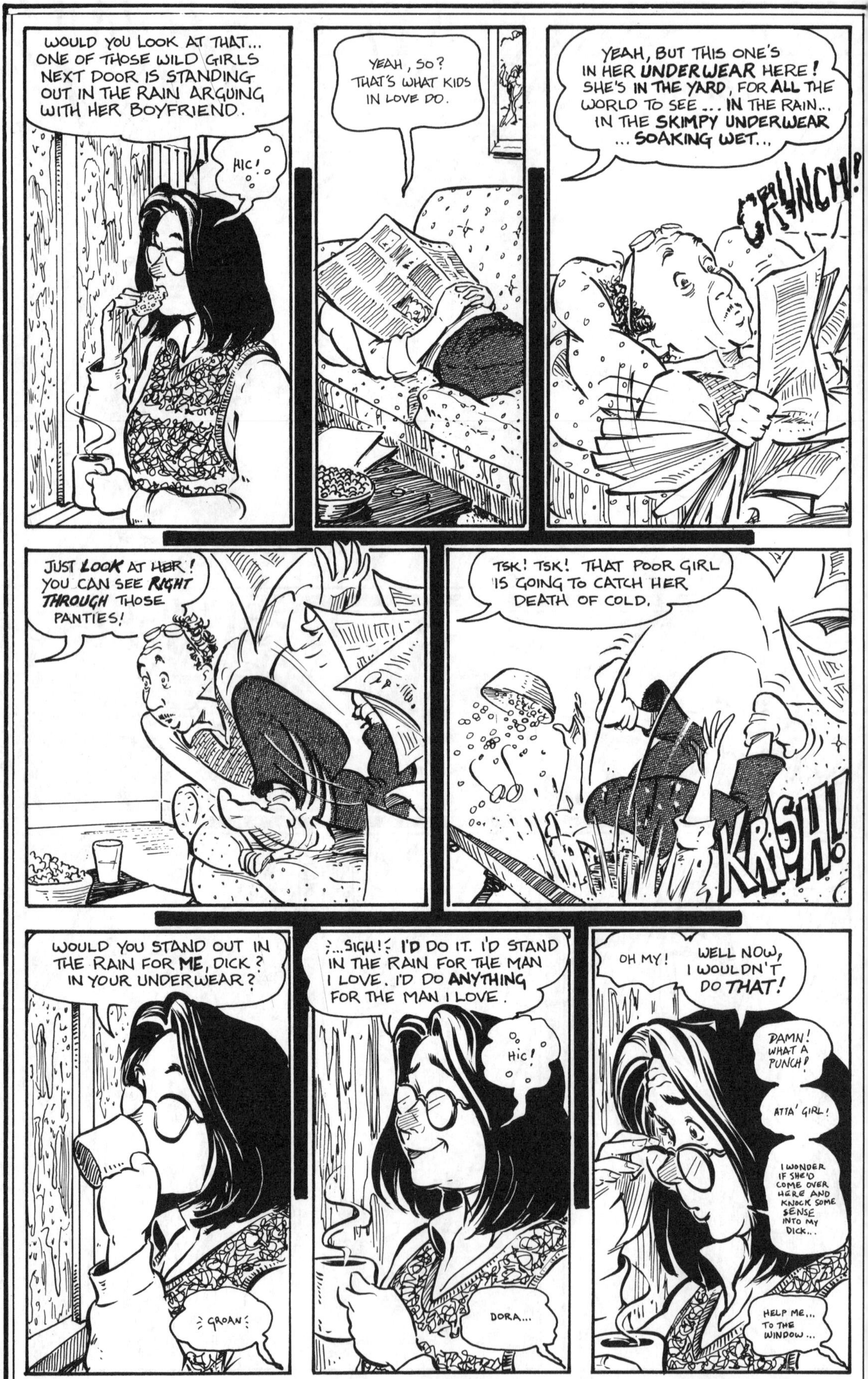
WOULD YOU LOOK AT THAT... ONE OF THOSE WILD GIRLS NEXT DOOR IS STANDING OUT IN THE RAIN ARGUING WITH HER BOYFRIEND.
HIC!
YEAH, SO? THAT'S WHAT KIDS IN LOVE DO.
YEAH, BUT THIS ONE'S IN HER UNDERWEAR HERE! SHE'S IN THE YARD, FOR ALL THE WORLD TO SEE... IN THE RAIN... IN THE SKIMPY UNDERWEAR ...SOAKING WET...
CRUNCH!
JUST LOOK AT HER! YOU CAN SEE RIGHT THROUGH THOSE PANTIES!
TSK! TSK! THAT POOR GIRL IS GOING TO CATCH HER DEATH OF COLD.
KRASH!
WOULD YOU STAND OUT IN THE RAIN FOR ME, DICK? IN YOUR UNDERWEAR?
GROAN
...SIGH! I'D DO IT. I'D STAND IN THE RAIN FOR THE MAN I LOVE. I'D DO ANYTHING FOR THE MAN I LOVE.
HIC!
DORA...
OH MY!
WELL NOW, I WOULDN'T DO THAT!
DAMN! WHAT A PUNCH!
ATTA' GIRL!
I WONDER IF SHE'D COME OVER HERE AND KNOCK SOME SENSE INTO MY DICK...
HELP ME... TO THE WINDOW...

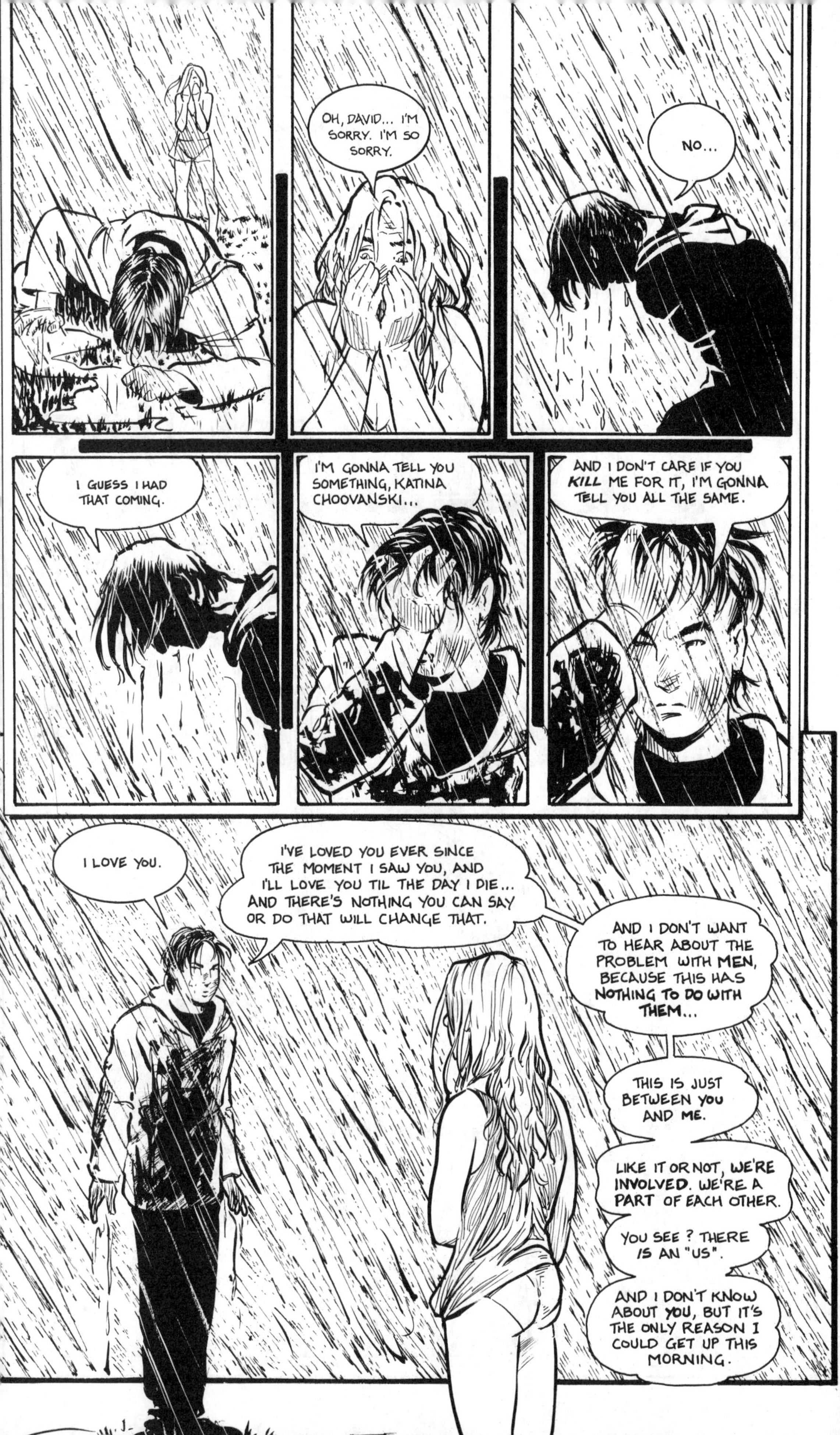
OH, DAVID... I'M SORRY. I'M SO SORRY.
NO...
I GUESS I HAD THAT COMING.
I'M GONNA TELL YOU SOMETHING, KATINA CHOOVANSKI...
AND I DON'T CARE IF YOU KILL ME FOR IT, I'M GONNA TELL YOU ALL THE SAME.
I LOVE YOU.
I'VE LOVED YOU EVER SINCE THE MOMENT I SAW YOU, AND I'LL LOVE YOU TIL THE DAY I DIE... AND THERE'S NOTHING YOU CAN SAY OR DO THAT WILL CHANGE THAT.
AND I DON'T WANT TO HEAR ABOUT THE PROBLEM WITH MEN, BECAUSE THIS HAS NOTHING TO DO WITH THEM...
THIS IS JUST BETWEEN YOU AND ME.
LIKE IT OR NOT, WE'RE INVOLVED. WE'RE A PART OF EACH OTHER.
YOU SEE? THERE IS AN "US".
AND I DON'T KNOW ABOUT YOU, BUT IT'S THE ONLY REASON I COULD GET UP THIS MORNING.

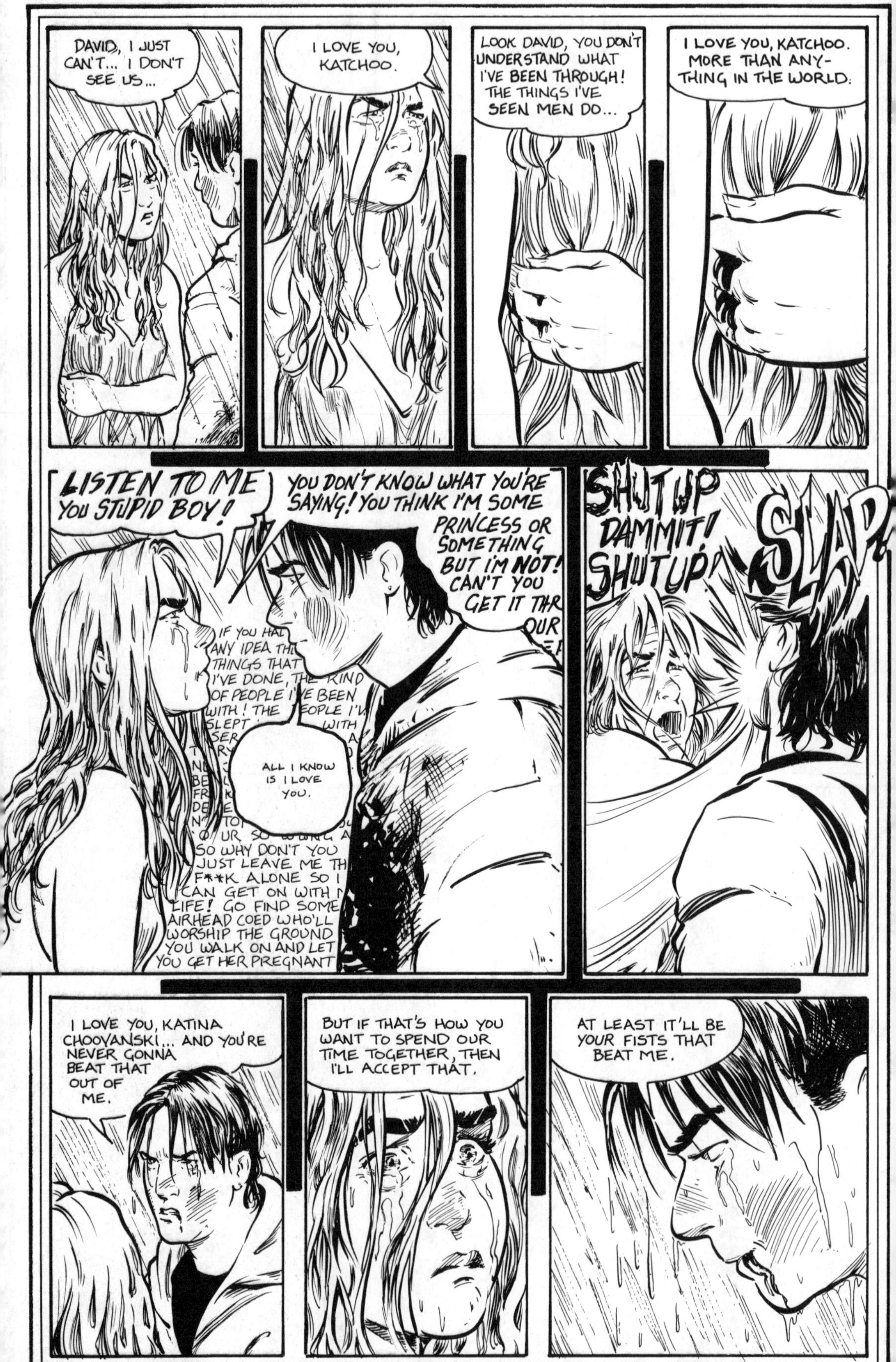
DAVID, I JUST CAN'T... I DON'T SEE US...
I LOVE YOU, KATCHOO.
LOOK DAVID, YOU DON'T UNDERSTAND WHAT I'VE BEEN THROUGH! THE THINGS I'VE SEEN MEN DO...
I LOVE YOU, KATCHOO. MORE THAN ANY-THING IN THE WORLD.
LISTEN TO ME YOU STUPID BOY!
YOU DON'T KNOW WHAT YOU'RE SAYING! YOU THINK I'M SOME PRINCESS OR SOMETHING BUT I'M NOT! CAN'T YOU GET IT THR
IF YOU HA ANY IDEA TH THINGS THAT I'VE DONE, THE KIND OF PEOPLE I'VE BEEN WITH! THE PEOPLE I'V SLEPT WITH
SO WHY DON'T YOU JUST LEAVE ME TH F**K ALONE SO I CAN GET ON WITH LIFE! GO FIND SOME AIRHEAD COED WHO'LL WORSHIP THE GROUND YOU WALK ON AND LET YOU GET HER PREGNANT
ALL I KNOW IS I LOVE YOU.
SHUT UP DAMMIT! SHUT UP!
SLAP!
I LOVE YOU, KATINA CHOOVANSKI... AND YOU'RE NEVER GONNA BEAT THAT OUT OF ME.
BUT IF THAT'S HOW YOU WANT TO SPEND OUR TIME TOGETHER, THEN I'LL ACCEPT THAT.
AT LEAST IT'LL BE YOUR FISTS THAT BEAT ME.

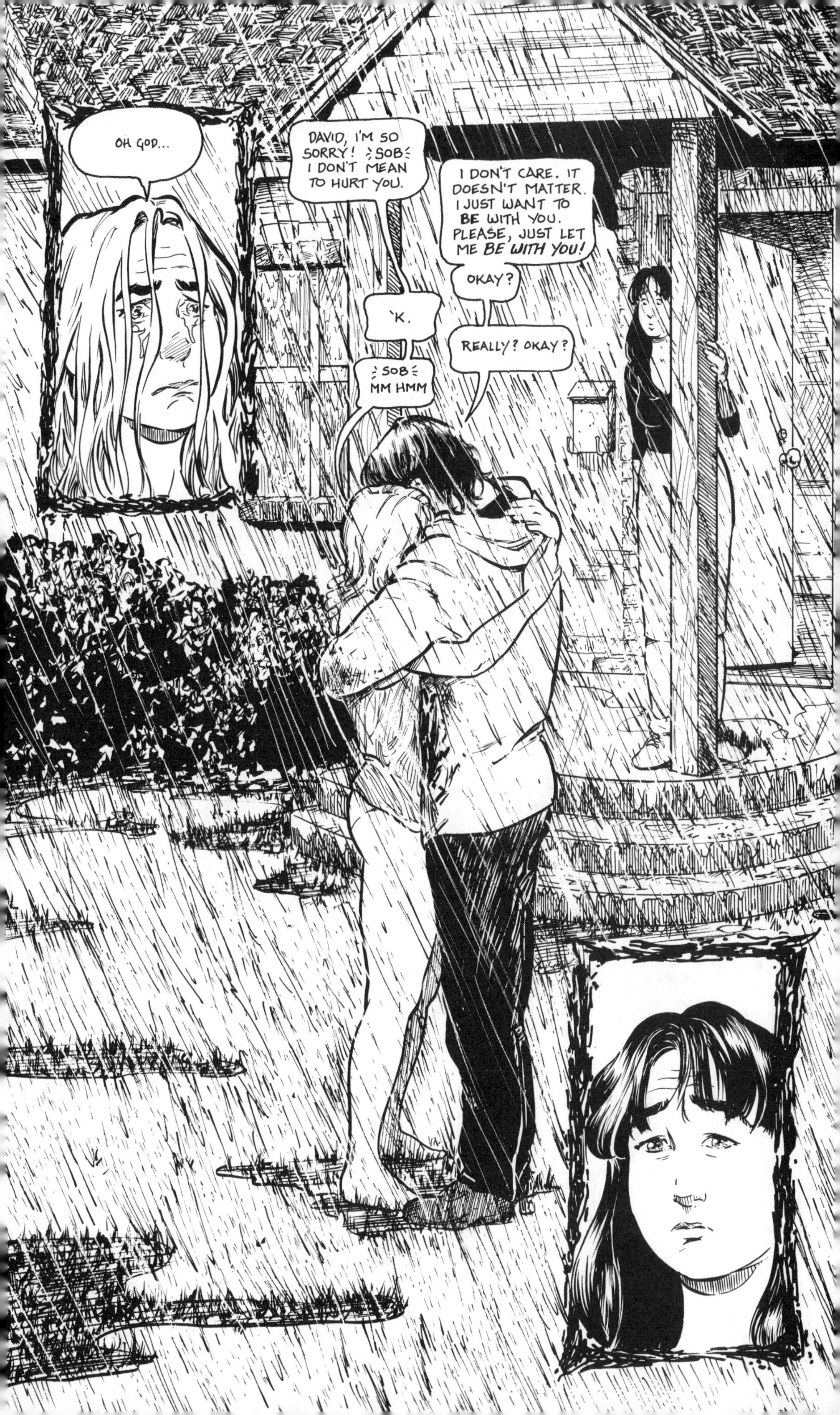
OH GOD...
DAVID, I'M SO SORRY! SOB I DON'T MEAN TO HURT YOU.
I DON'T CARE. IT DOESN'T MATTER. I JUST WANT TO BE WITH YOU. PLEASE, JUST LET ME BE WITH YOU!
OKAY?
`K.
REALLY? OKAY?
SOB MM HMM

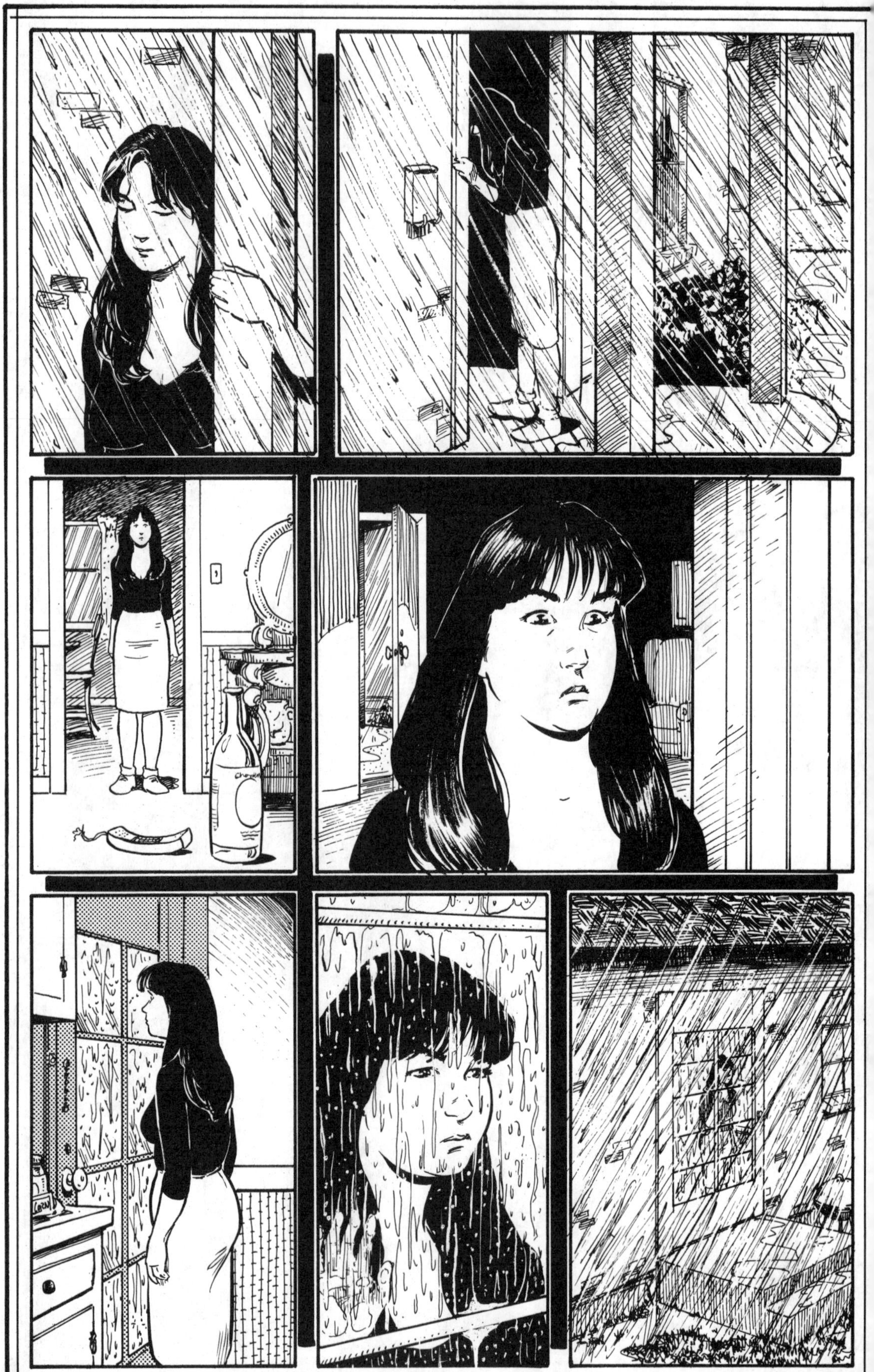

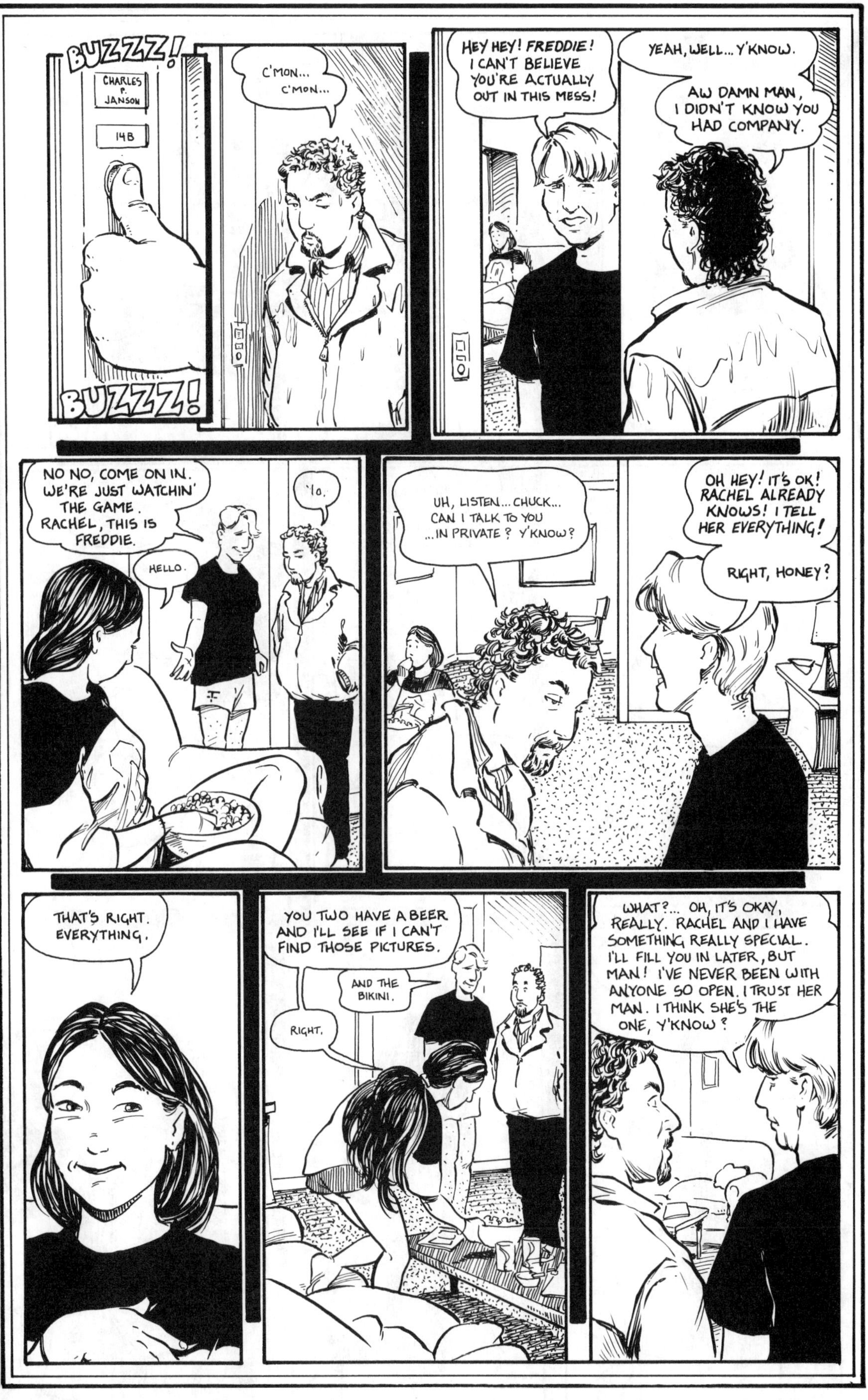
BUZZZ!
CHARLES P. JANSON
14B
BUZZZ!
C'MON... C'MON...
HEY HEY! FREDDIE! I CAN'T BELIEVE YOU'RE ACTUALLY OUT IN THIS MESS!
YEAH, WELL... Y'KNOW.
AW DAMN MAN, I DIDN'T KNOW YOU HAD COMPANY.
NO NO, COME ON IN. WE'RE JUST WATCHIN' THE GAME. RACHEL, THIS IS FREDDIE.
'lo.
HELLO.
UH, LISTEN... CHUCK... CAN I TALK TO YOU ...IN PRIVATE? Y'KNOW?
OH HEY! IT'S OK! RACHEL ALREADY KNOWS! I TELL HER EVERYTHING!
RIGHT, HONEY?
THAT'S RIGHT. EVERYTHING.
YOU TWO HAVE A BEER AND I'LL SEE IF I CAN'T FIND THOSE PICTURES.
AND THE BIKINI.
RIGHT.
WHAT?... OH, IT'S OKAY, REALLY. RACHEL AND I HAVE SOMETHING REALLY SPECIAL. I'LL FILL YOU IN LATER, BUT MAN! I'VE NEVER BEEN WITH ANYONE SO OPEN. I TRUST HER MAN. I THINK SHE'S THE ONE, Y'KNOW?

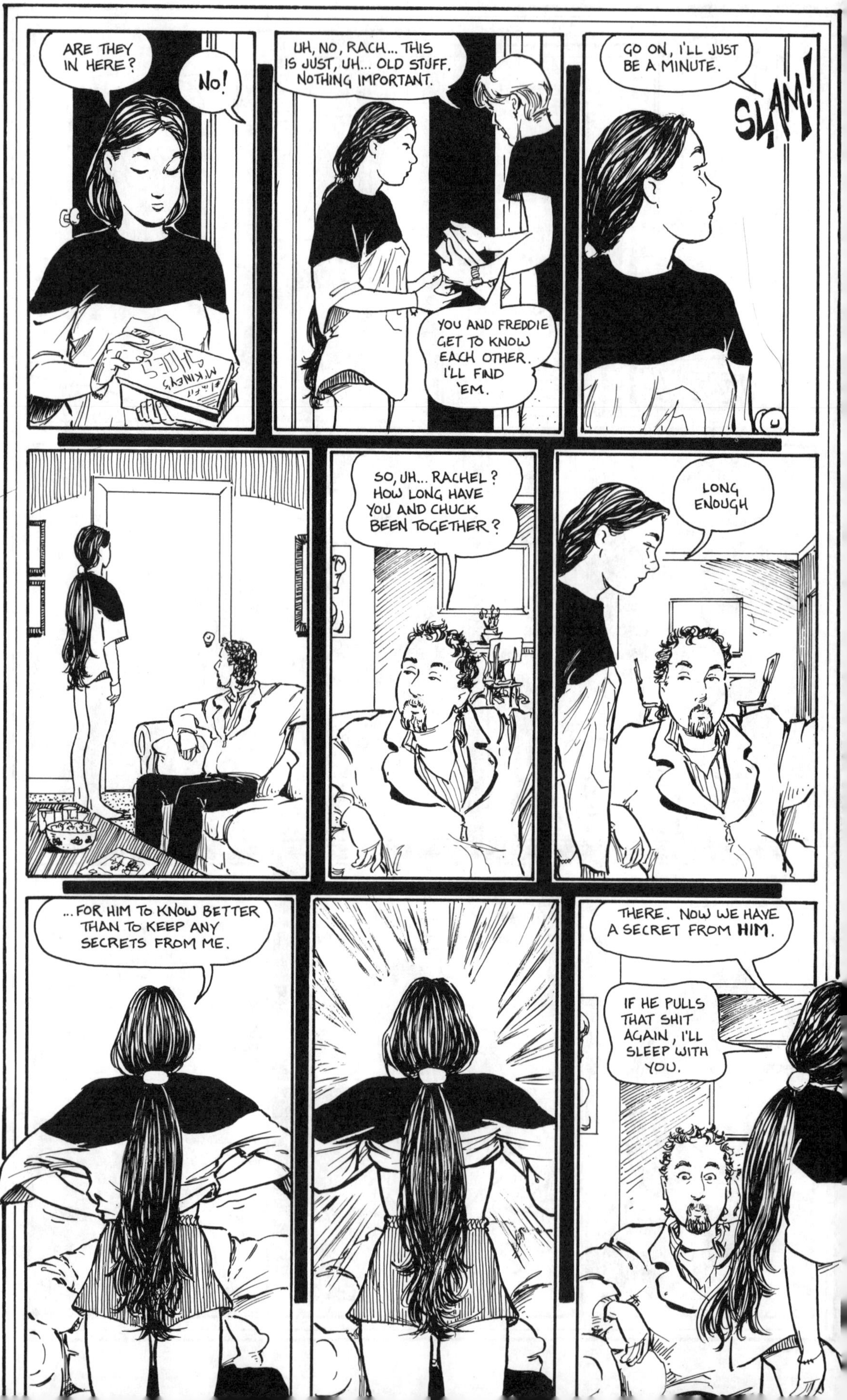

ARE THEY IN HERE?
No!
#1 FIT M^CKINEY'S SHOES
UH, NO, RACH... THIS IS JUST, UH... OLD STUFF. NOTHING IMPORTANT.
YOU AND FREDDIE GET TO KNOW EACH OTHER. I'LL FIND 'EM.
GO ON, I'LL JUST BE A MINUTE.
SLAM!
SO, UH... RACHEL? HOW LONG HAVE YOU AND CHUCK BEEN TOGETHER?
LONG ENOUGH
...FOR HIM TO KNOW BETTER THAN TO KEEP ANY SECRETS FROM ME.
THERE. NOW WE HAVE A SECRET FROM **HIM**.
IF HE PULLS THAT SHIT AGAIN, I'LL SLEEP WITH YOU.

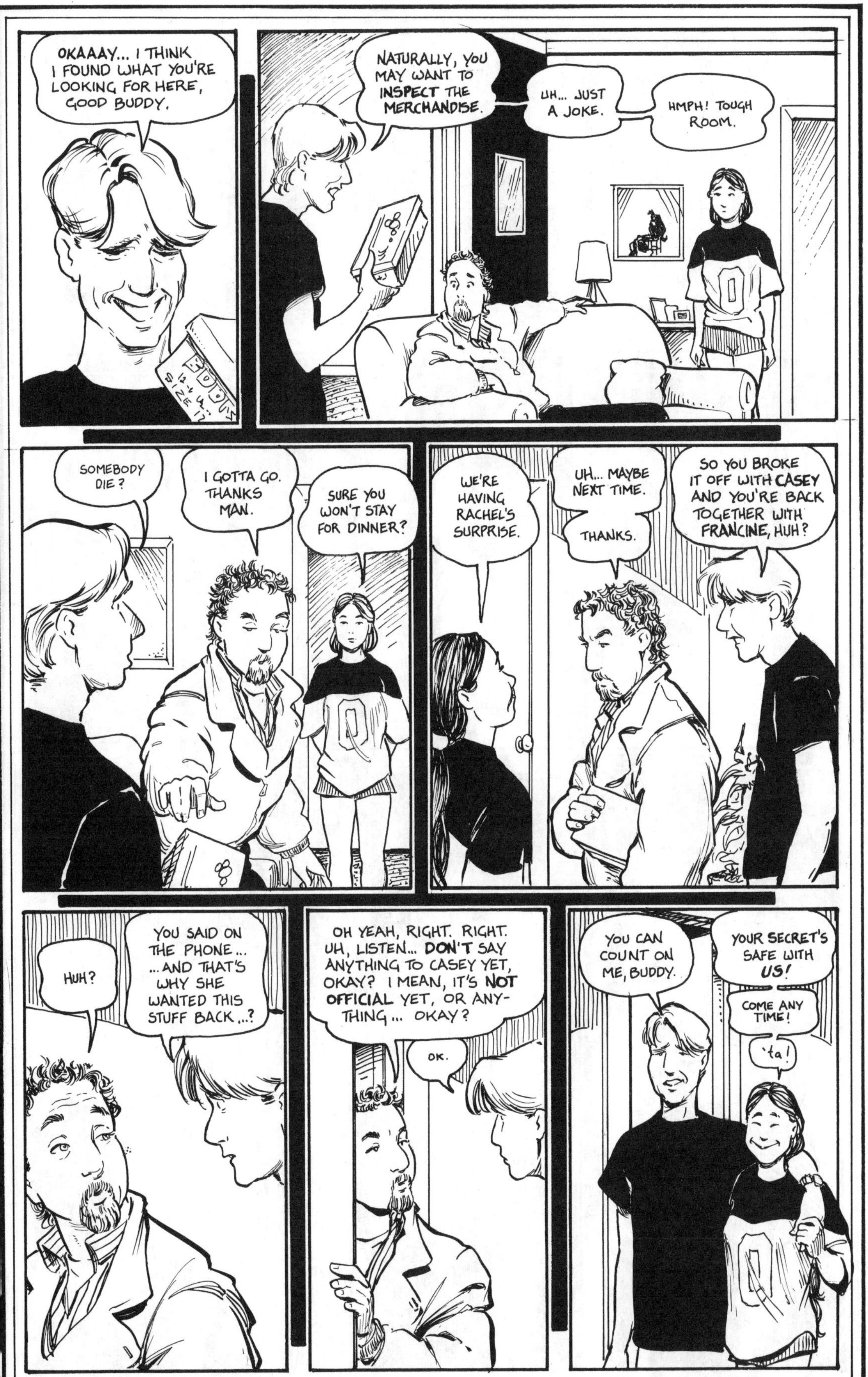
OKAAAY... I THINK I FOUND WHAT YOU'RE LOOKING FOR HERE, GOOD BUDDY.
NATURALLY, YOU MAY WANT TO INSPECT THE MERCHANDISE.
UH... JUST A JOKE.
HMPH! TOUGH ROOM.
SOMEBODY DIE?
I GOTTA GO. THANKS MAN.
SURE YOU WON'T STAY FOR DINNER?
WE'RE HAVING RACHEL'S SURPRISE.
UH... MAYBE NEXT TIME.
THANKS.
SO YOU BROKE IT OFF WITH CASEY AND YOU'RE BACK TOGETHER WITH FRANCINE, HUH?
HUH?
YOU SAID ON THE PHONE... ...AND THAT'S WHY SHE WANTED THIS STUFF BACK...?
OH YEAH, RIGHT. RIGHT. UH, LISTEN... DON'T SAY ANYTHING TO CASEY YET, OKAY? I MEAN, IT'S NOT OFFICIAL YET, OR ANYTHING... OKAY?
OK.
YOU CAN COUNT ON ME, BUDDY.
YOUR SECRET'S SAFE WITH US!
COME ANY TIME!
'ta!

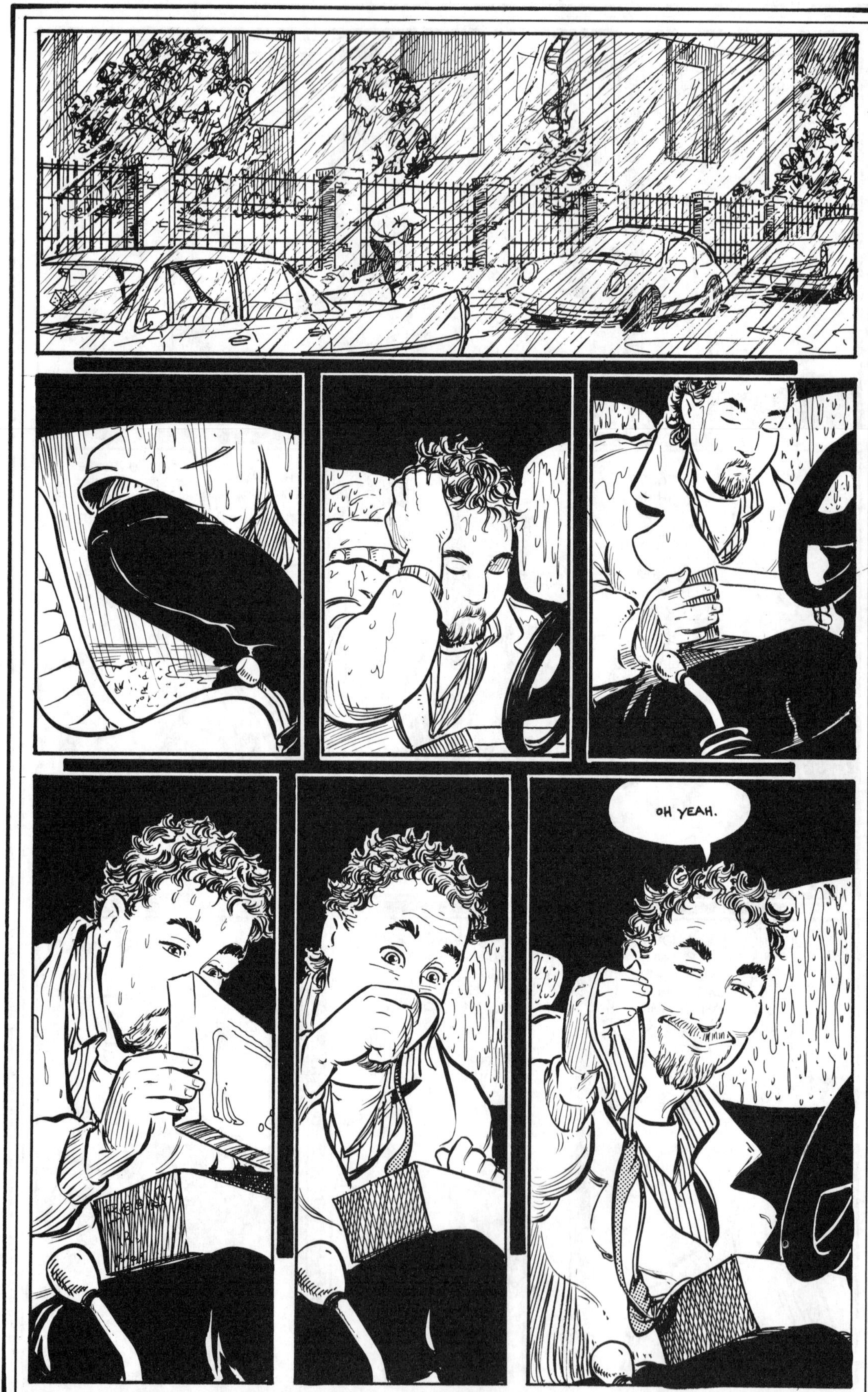
OH YEAH.

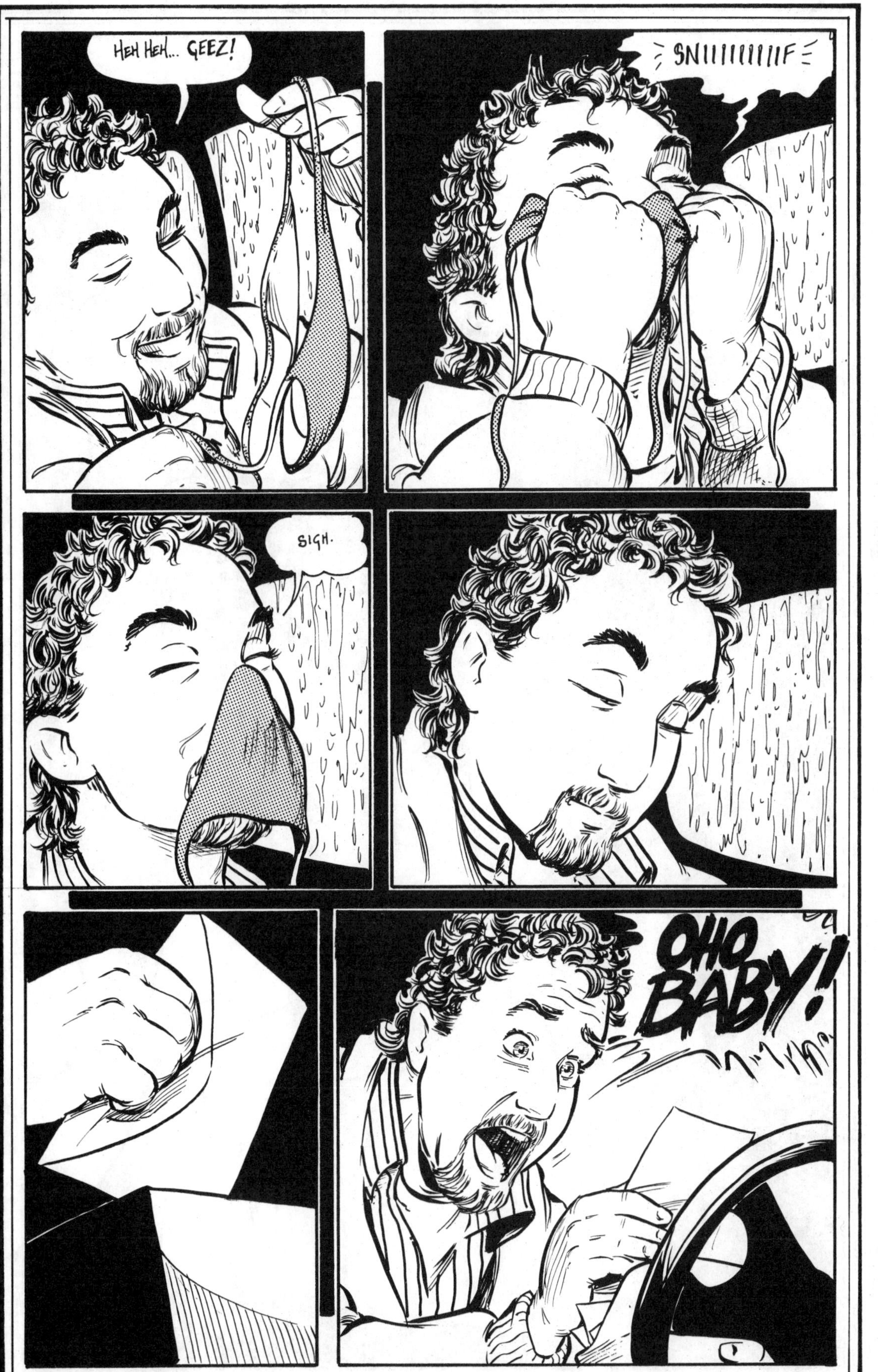
HEH HEH... GEEZ!
SNIIIIIIIIIF
SIGH.
OHO BABY!

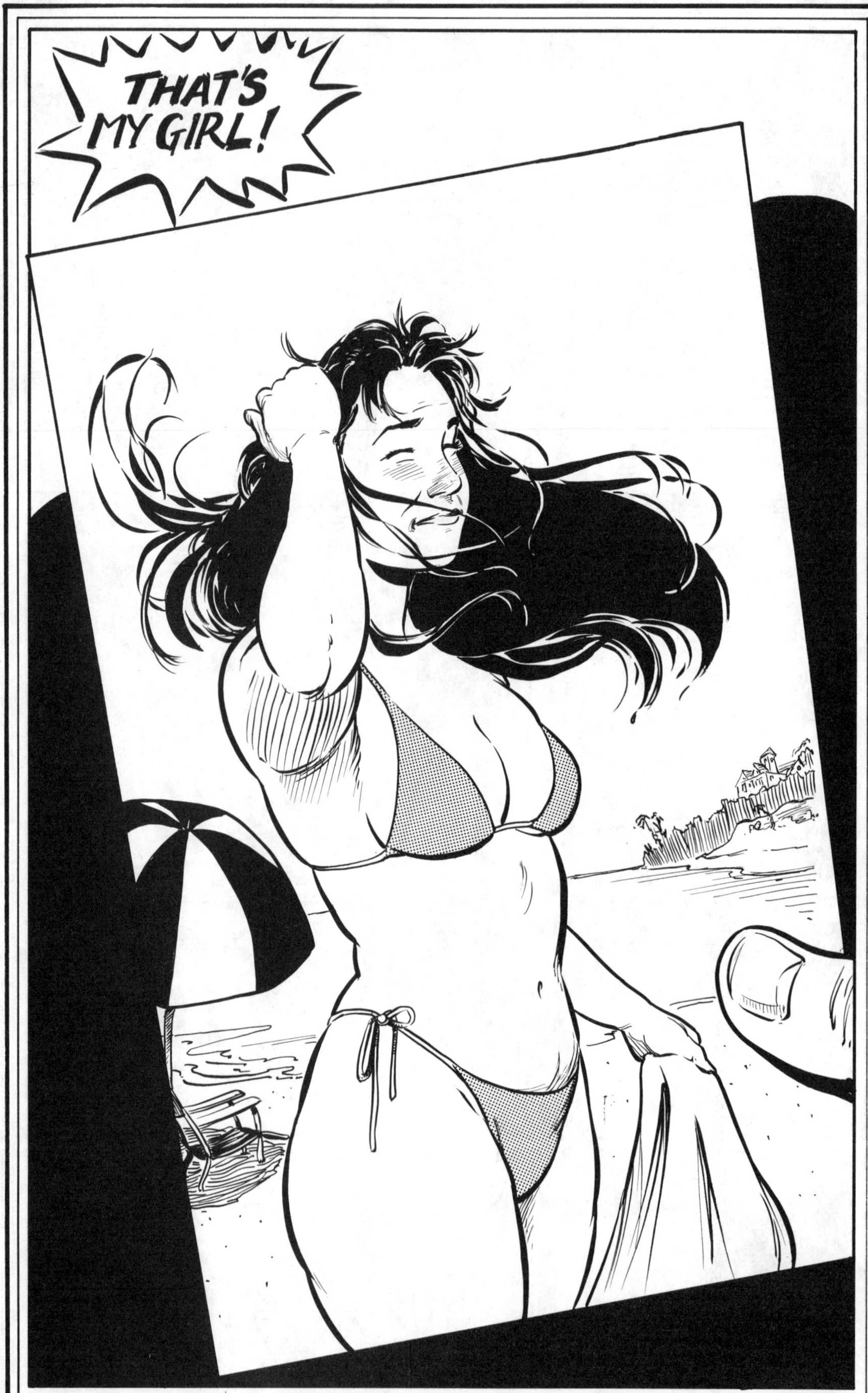
THAT'S MY GIRL!

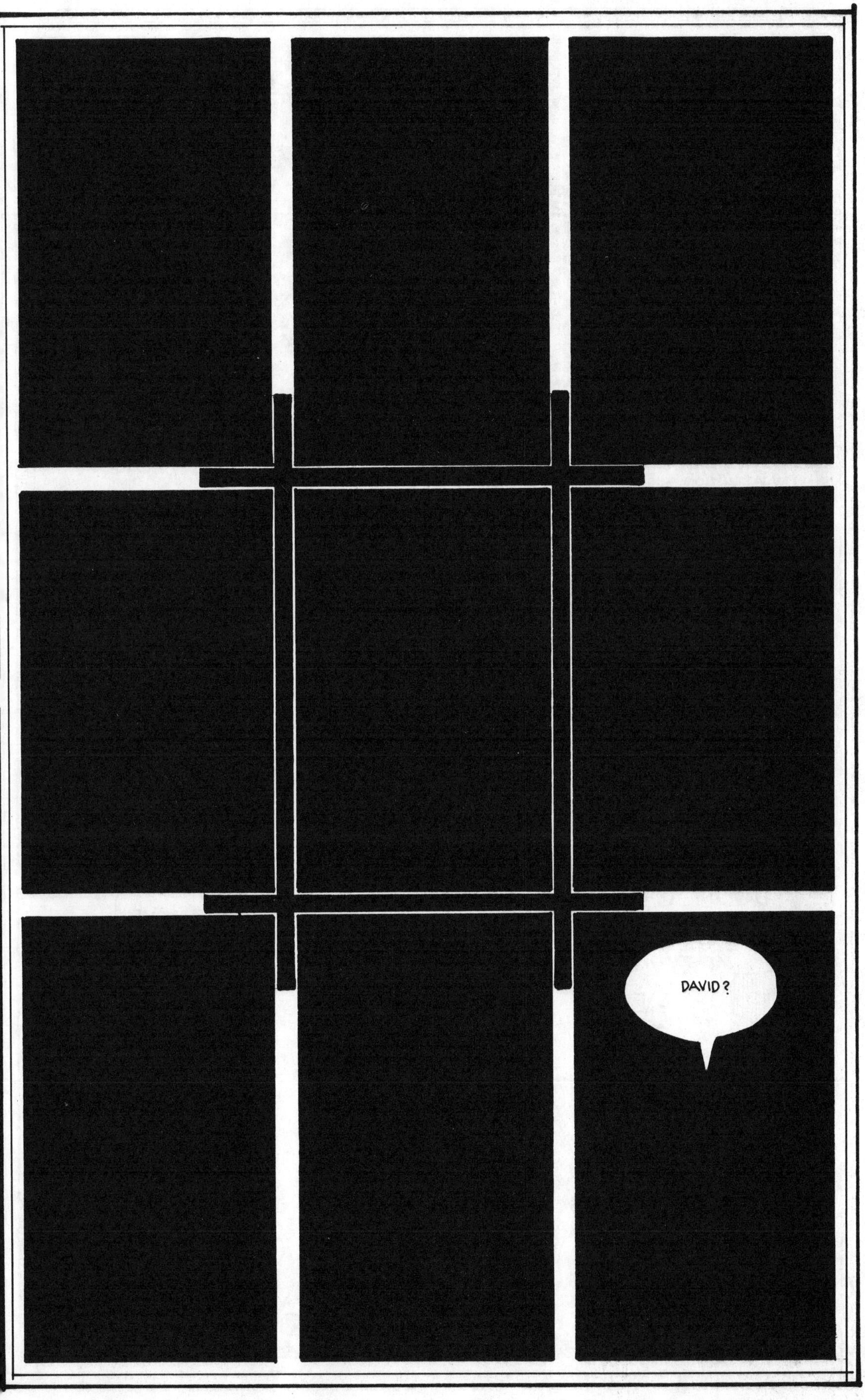
DAVID?

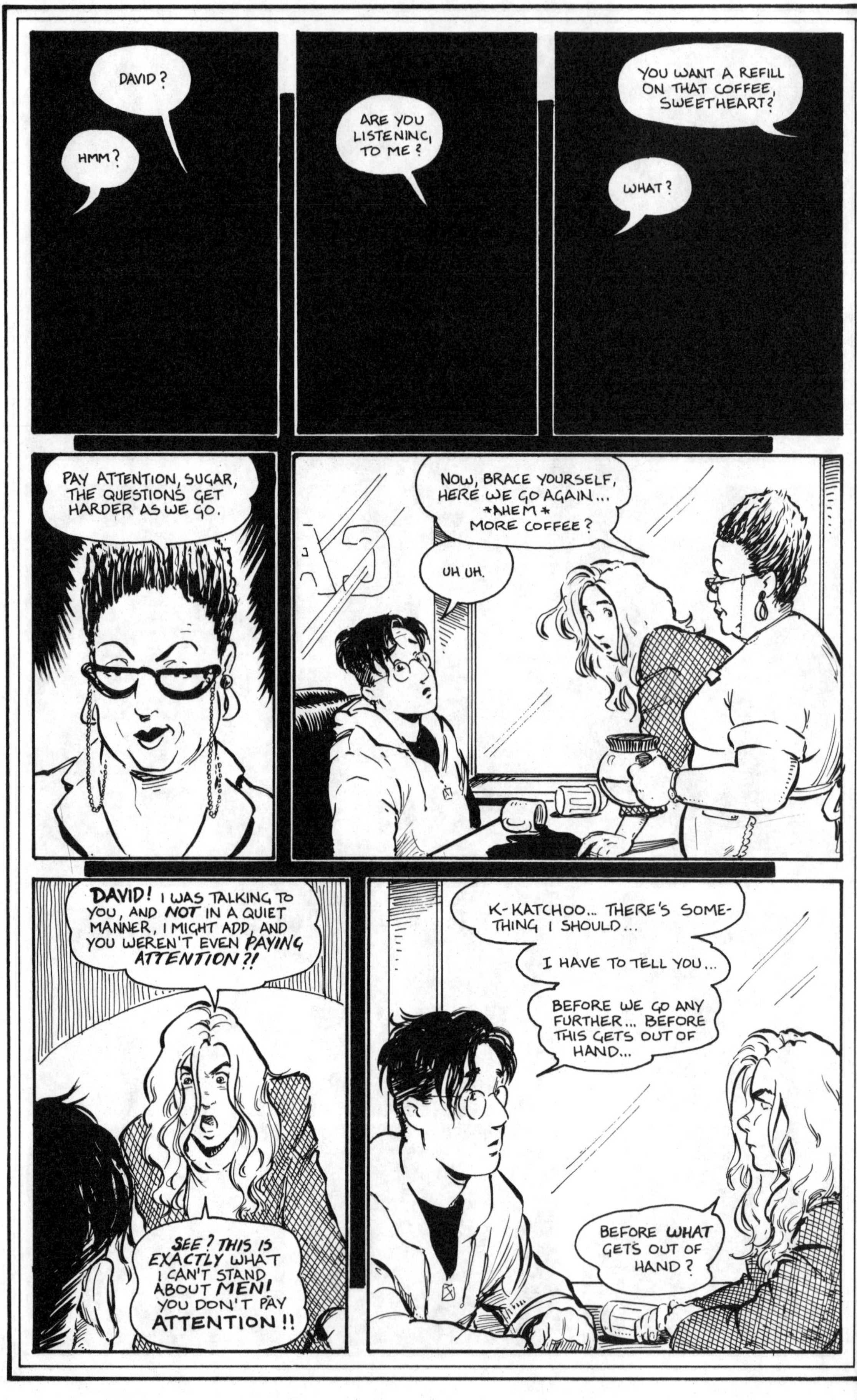
DAVID?
HMM?
ARE YOU LISTENING, TO ME?
YOU WANT A REFILL ON THAT COFFEE, SWEETHEART?
WHAT?
PAY ATTENTION, SUGAR, THE QUESTIONS GET HARDER AS WE GO.
NOW, BRACE YOURSELF, HERE WE GO AGAIN... *AHEM* MORE COFFEE?
UH UH.
DAVID! I WAS TALKING TO YOU, AND NOT IN A QUIET MANNER, I MIGHT ADD, AND YOU WEREN'T EVEN PAYING ATTENTION?!
SEE? THIS IS EXACTLY WHAT I CAN'T STAND ABOUT MEN! YOU DON'T PAY ATTENTION!!
K-KATCHOO... THERE'S SOMETHING I SHOULD...
I HAVE TO TELL YOU...
BEFORE WE GO ANY FURTHER... BEFORE THIS GETS OUT OF HAND...
BEFORE WHAT GETS OUT OF HAND?

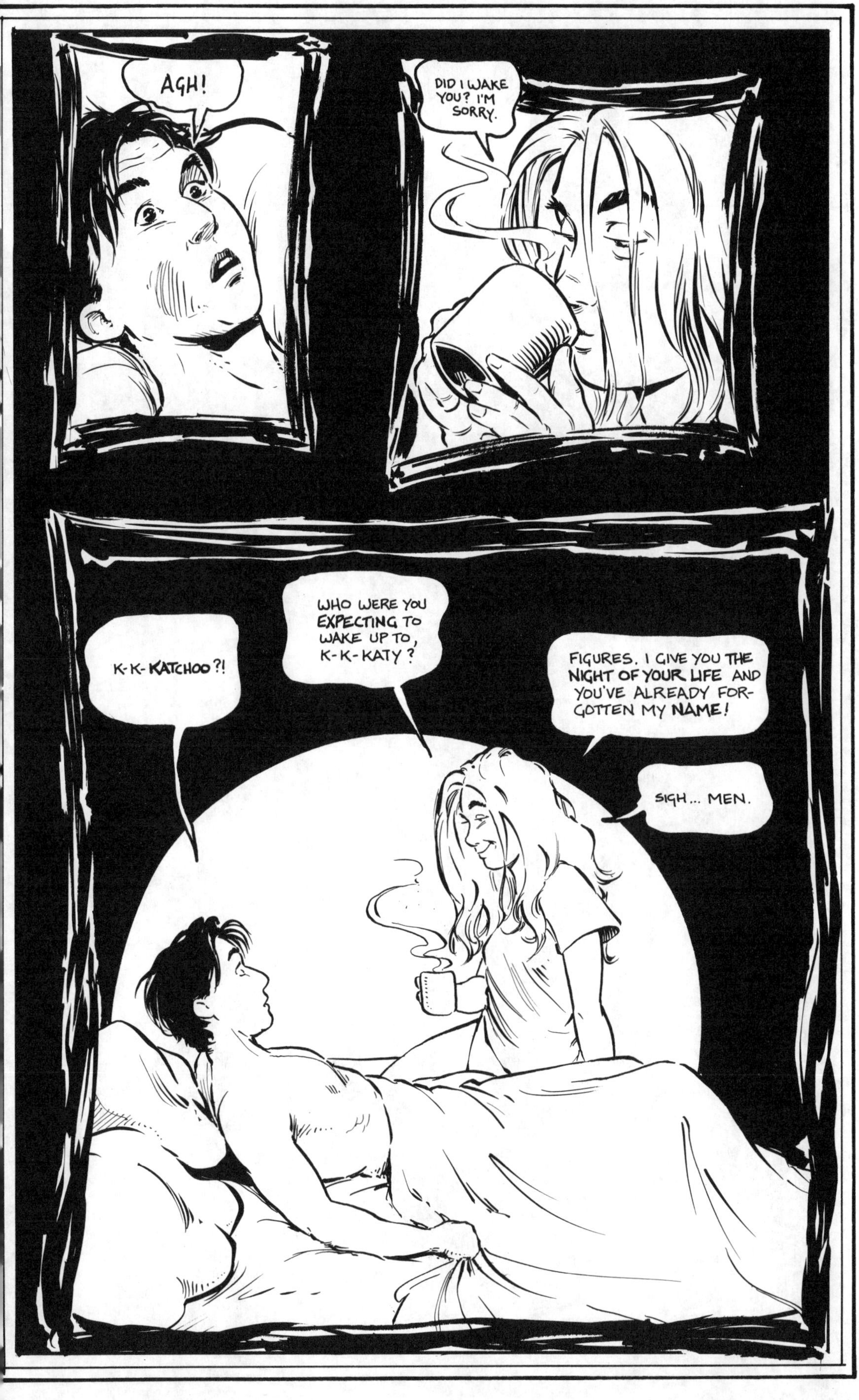
AGH!
DID I WAKE YOU? I'M SORRY.
K-K-KATCHOO?!
WHO WERE YOU EXPECTING TO WAKE UP TO, K-K-KATY?
FIGURES. I GIVE YOU THE NIGHT OF YOUR LIFE AND YOU'VE ALREADY FORGOTTEN MY NAME!
SIGH... MEN.

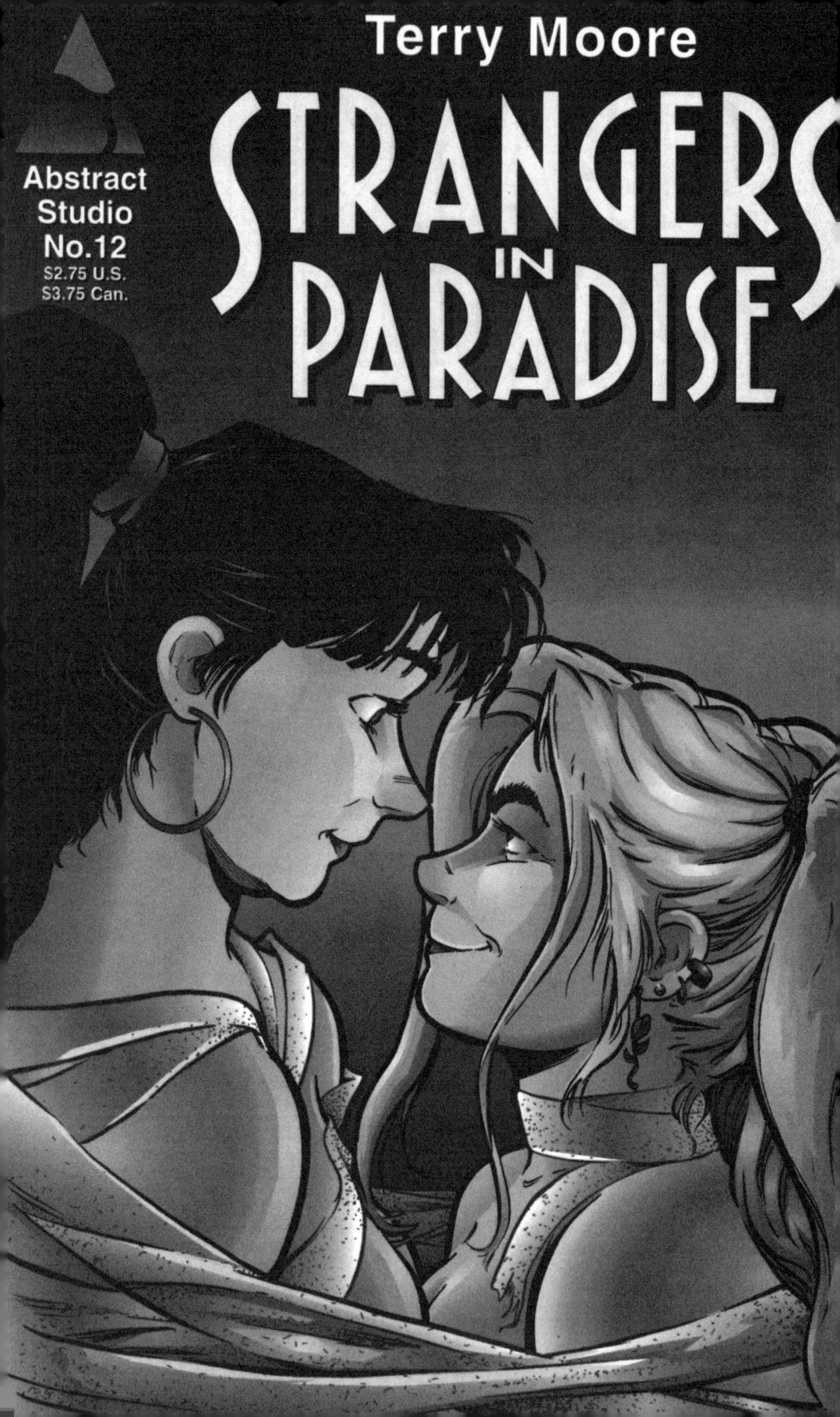
Terry Moore
STRANGERS IN PARADISE
Abstract Studio
No.12
$2.75 U.S.
$3.75 Can.

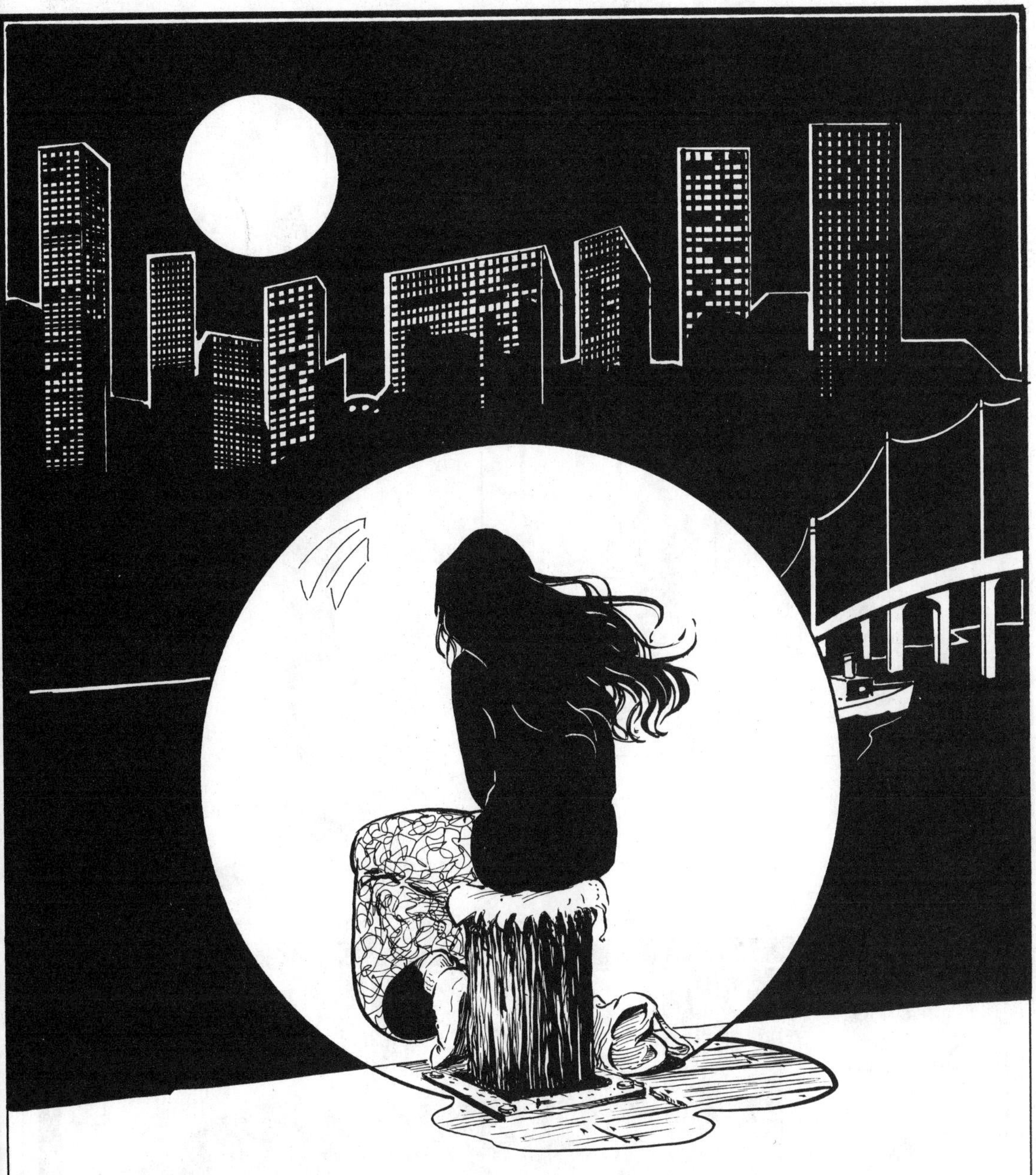

If you're leaving me
please don't tell me
You're still pleasing me
Do I fail you
I will wonder today
if tomorrow you'll stay
I can hear your voice turn cold
when you turn to me I know
I'm the one who won't let go
Are you blaming me
for holding on
when you let me know
it's my last chance
And I know it's gone

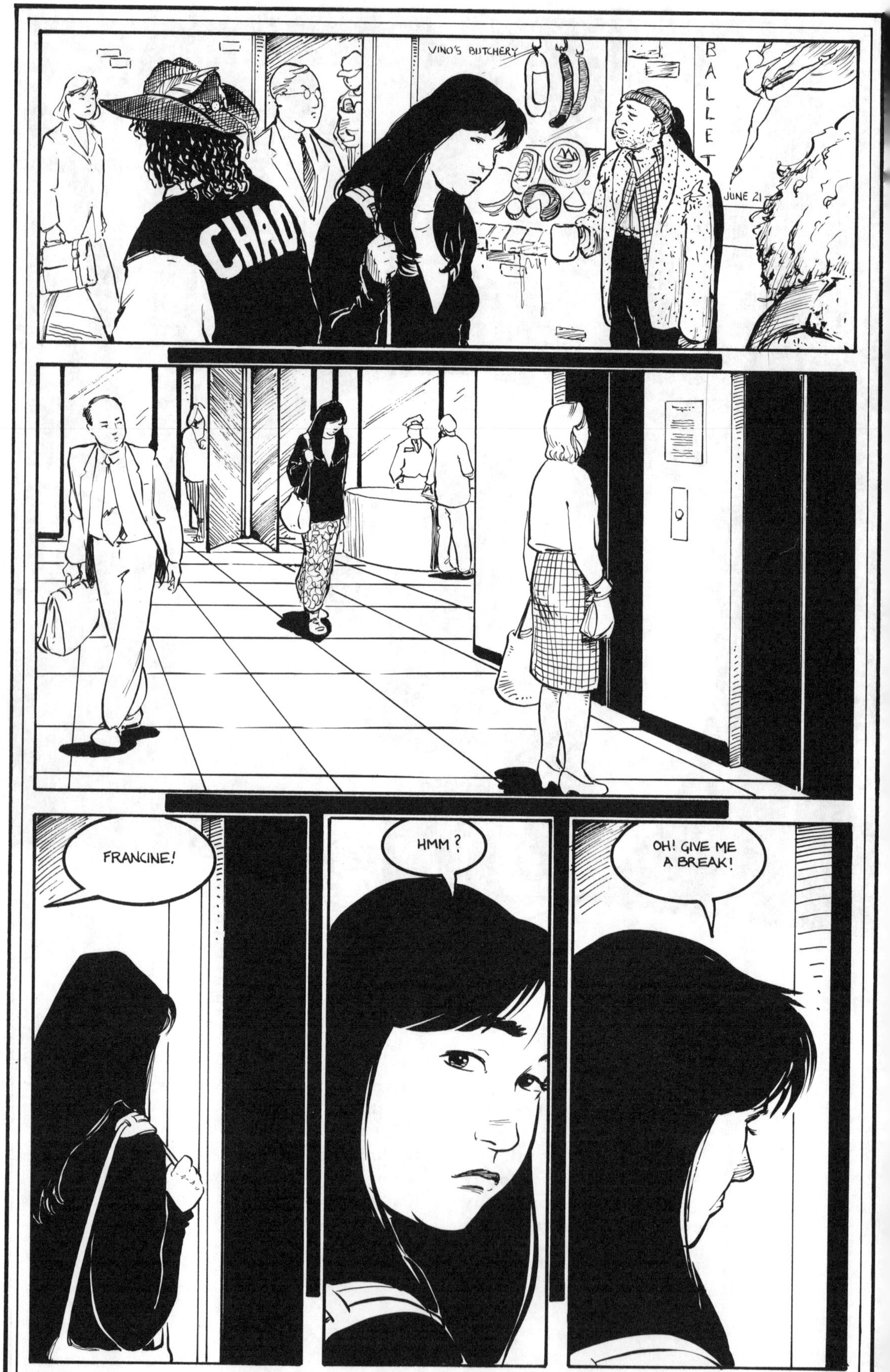
VINO'S BUTCHERY
CHAD
BALLET
JUNE 21
FRANCINE!
HMM ?
OH! GIVE ME A BREAK!

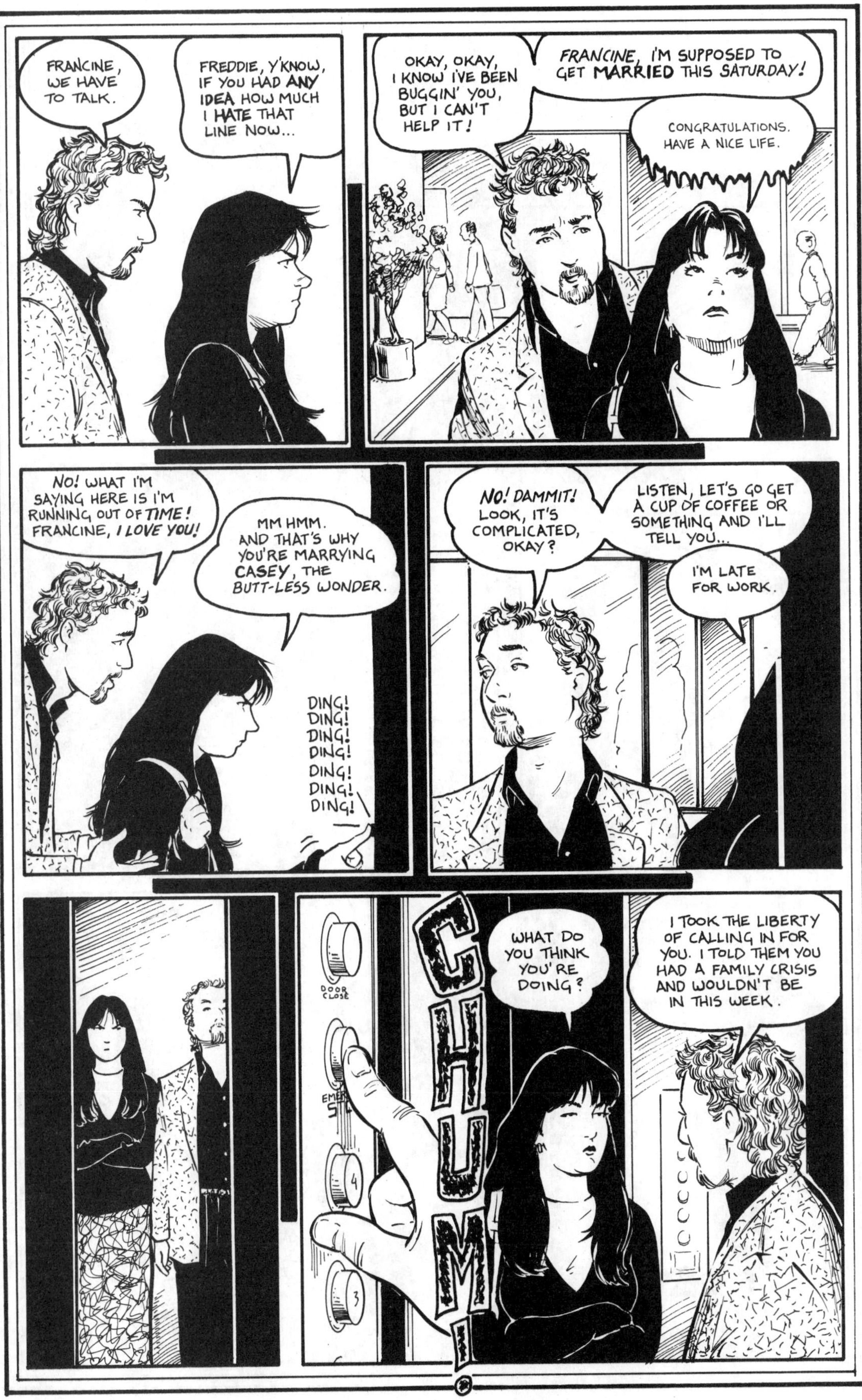
FRANCINE, WE HAVE TO TALK.
FREDDIE, Y'KNOW, IF YOU HAD ANY IDEA HOW MUCH I HATE THAT LINE NOW...
OKAY, OKAY, I KNOW I'VE BEEN BUGGIN' YOU, BUT I CAN'T HELP IT!
FRANCINE, I'M SUPPOSED TO GET MARRIED THIS SATURDAY!
CONGRATULATIONS. HAVE A NICE LIFE.
NO! WHAT I'M SAYING HERE IS I'M RUNNING OUT OF TIME! FRANCINE, I LOVE YOU!
MM HMM. AND THAT'S WHY YOU'RE MARRYING CASEY, THE BUTT-LESS WONDER.
DING! DING! DING! DING! DING! DING! DING!
NO! DAMMIT! LOOK, IT'S COMPLICATED, OKAY?
LISTEN, LET'S GO GET A CUP OF COFFEE OR SOMETHING AND I'LL TELL YOU...
I'M LATE FOR WORK.
DOOR CLOSE
CHUNM!
WHAT DO YOU THINK YOU'RE DOING?
I TOOK THE LIBERTY OF CALLING IN FOR YOU. I TOLD THEM YOU HAD A FAMILY CRISIS AND WOULDN'T BE IN THIS WEEK.

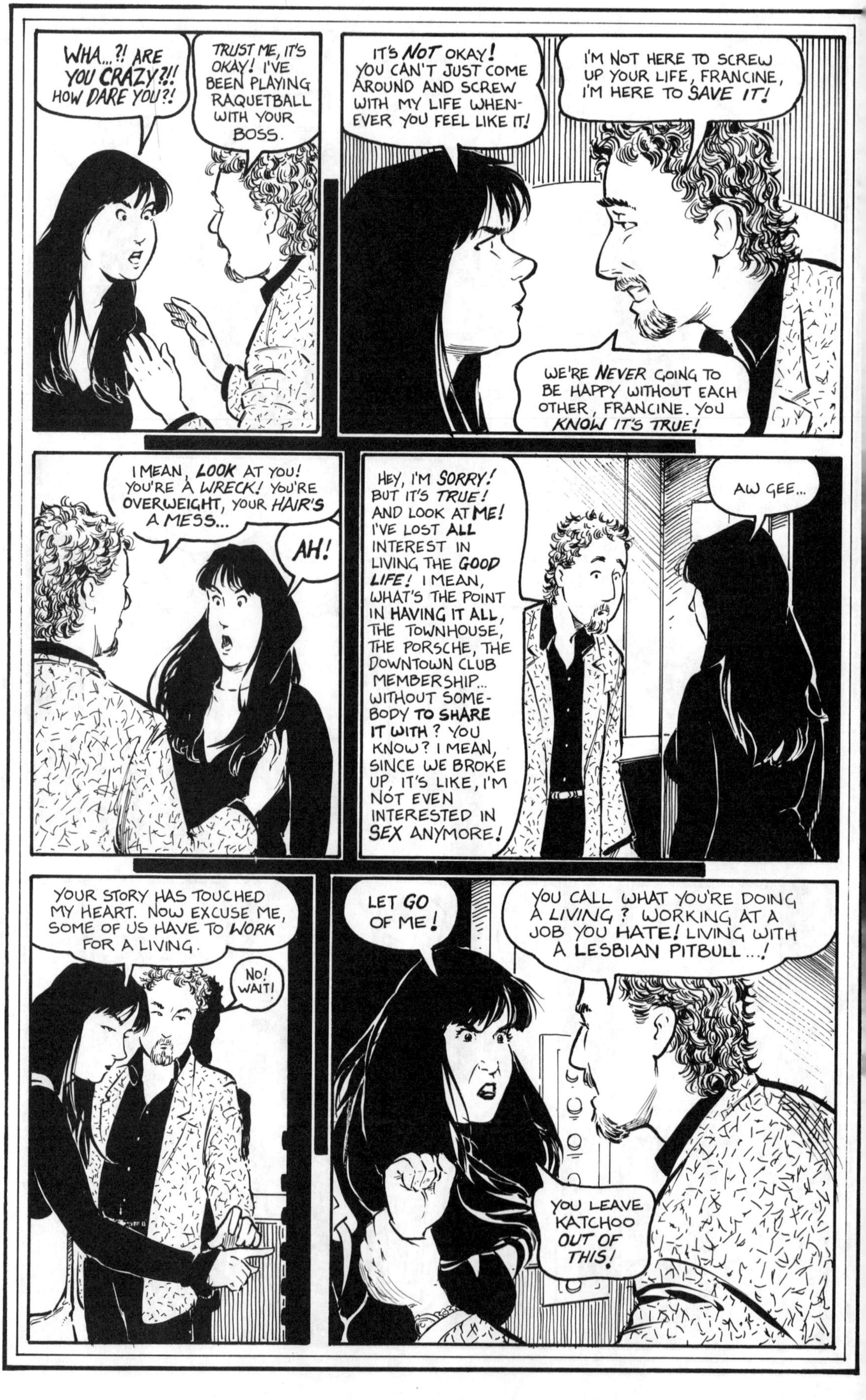
WHA...?! ARE YOU CRAZY?!! HOW DARE YOU?!
TRUST ME, IT'S OKAY! I'VE BEEN PLAYING RAQUETBALL WITH YOUR BOSS.
IT'S NOT OKAY! YOU CAN'T JUST COME AROUND AND SCREW WITH MY LIFE WHENEVER YOU FEEL LIKE IT!
I'M NOT HERE TO SCREW UP YOUR LIFE, FRANCINE, I'M HERE TO SAVE IT!
WE'RE NEVER GOING TO BE HAPPY WITHOUT EACH OTHER, FRANCINE. YOU KNOW IT'S TRUE!
I MEAN, LOOK AT YOU! YOU'RE A WRECK! YOU'RE OVERWEIGHT, YOUR HAIR'S A MESS...
AH!
HEY, I'M SORRY! BUT IT'S TRUE! AND LOOK AT ME! I'VE LOST ALL INTEREST IN LIVING THE GOOD LIFE! I MEAN, WHAT'S THE POINT IN HAVING IT ALL, THE TOWNHOUSE, THE PORSCHE, THE DOWNTOWN CLUB MEMBERSHIP... WITHOUT SOMEBODY TO SHARE IT WITH? YOU KNOW? I MEAN, SINCE WE BROKE UP, IT'S LIKE, I'M NOT EVEN INTERESTED IN SEX ANYMORE!
AW GEE...
YOUR STORY HAS TOUCHED MY HEART. NOW EXCUSE ME, SOME OF US HAVE TO WORK FOR A LIVING.
NO! WAIT!
LET GO OF ME!
YOU CALL WHAT YOU'RE DOING A LIVING? WORKING AT A JOB YOU HATE! LIVING WITH A LESBIAN PITBULL...!
YOU LEAVE KATCHOO OUT OF THIS!

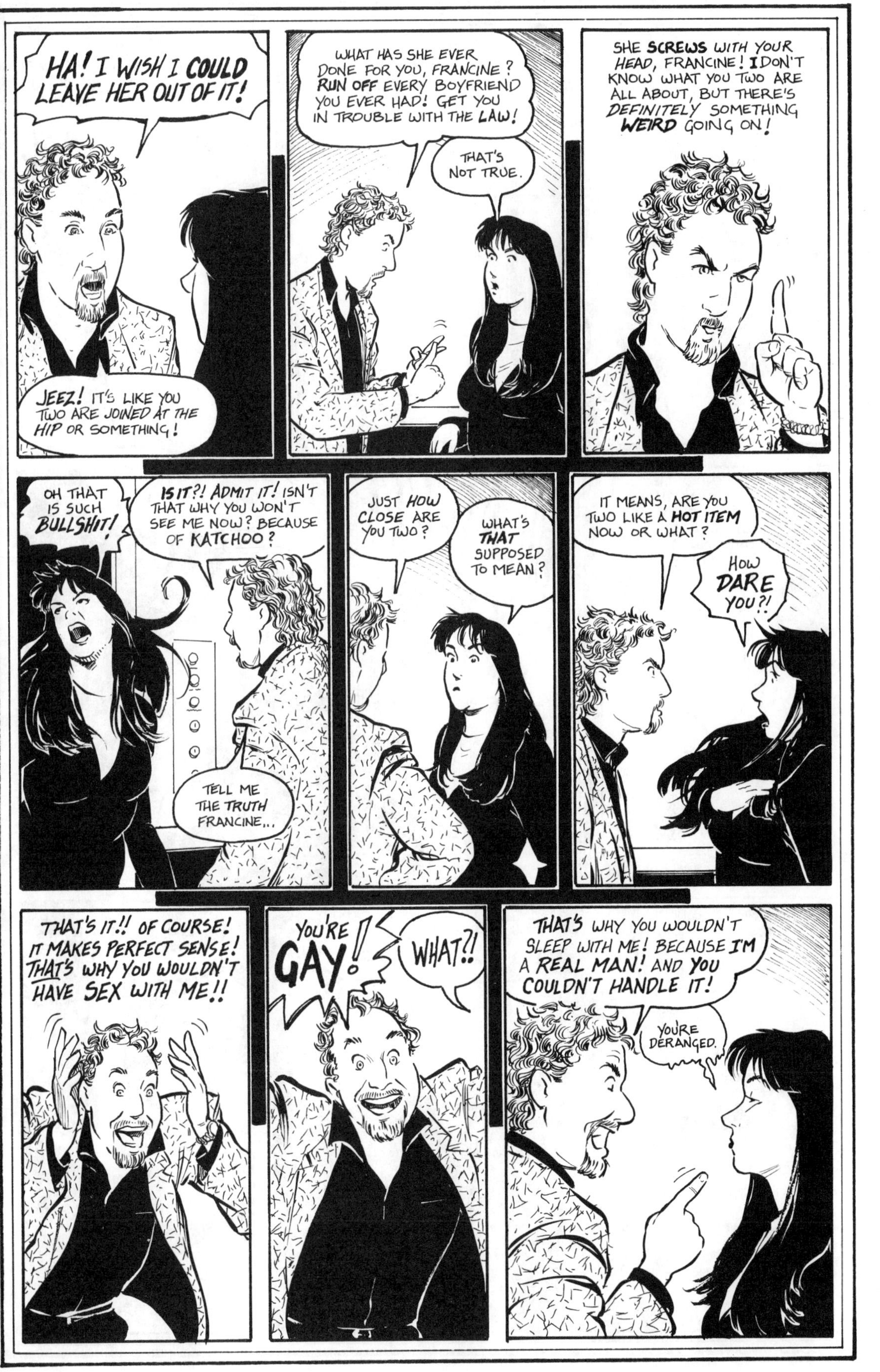
HA! I WISH I COULD LEAVE HER OUT OF IT!
JEEZ! IT'S LIKE YOU TWO ARE JOINED AT THE HIP OR SOMETHING!
WHAT HAS SHE EVER DONE FOR YOU, FRANCINE? RUN OFF EVERY BOYFRIEND YOU EVER HAD! GET YOU IN TROUBLE WITH THE LAW!
THAT'S NOT TRUE.
SHE SCREWS WITH YOUR HEAD, FRANCINE! I DON'T KNOW WHAT YOU TWO ARE ALL ABOUT, BUT THERE'S DEFINITELY SOMETHING WEIRD GOING ON!
OH THAT IS SUCH BULLSHIT!
IS IT?! ADMIT IT! ISN'T THAT WHY YOU WON'T SEE ME NOW? BECAUSE OF KATCHOO?
TELL ME THE TRUTH FRANCINE...
JUST HOW CLOSE ARE YOU TWO?
WHAT'S THAT SUPPOSED TO MEAN?
IT MEANS, ARE YOU TWO LIKE A HOT ITEM NOW OR WHAT?
HOW DARE YOU?!
THAT'S IT!! OF COURSE! IT MAKES PERFECT SENSE! THAT'S WHY YOU WOULDN'T HAVE SEX WITH ME!!
YOU'RE GAY!
WHAT?!
THAT'S WHY YOU WOULDN'T SLEEP WITH ME! BECAUSE I'M A REAL MAN! AND YOU COULDN'T HANDLE IT!
YOU'RE DERANGED.

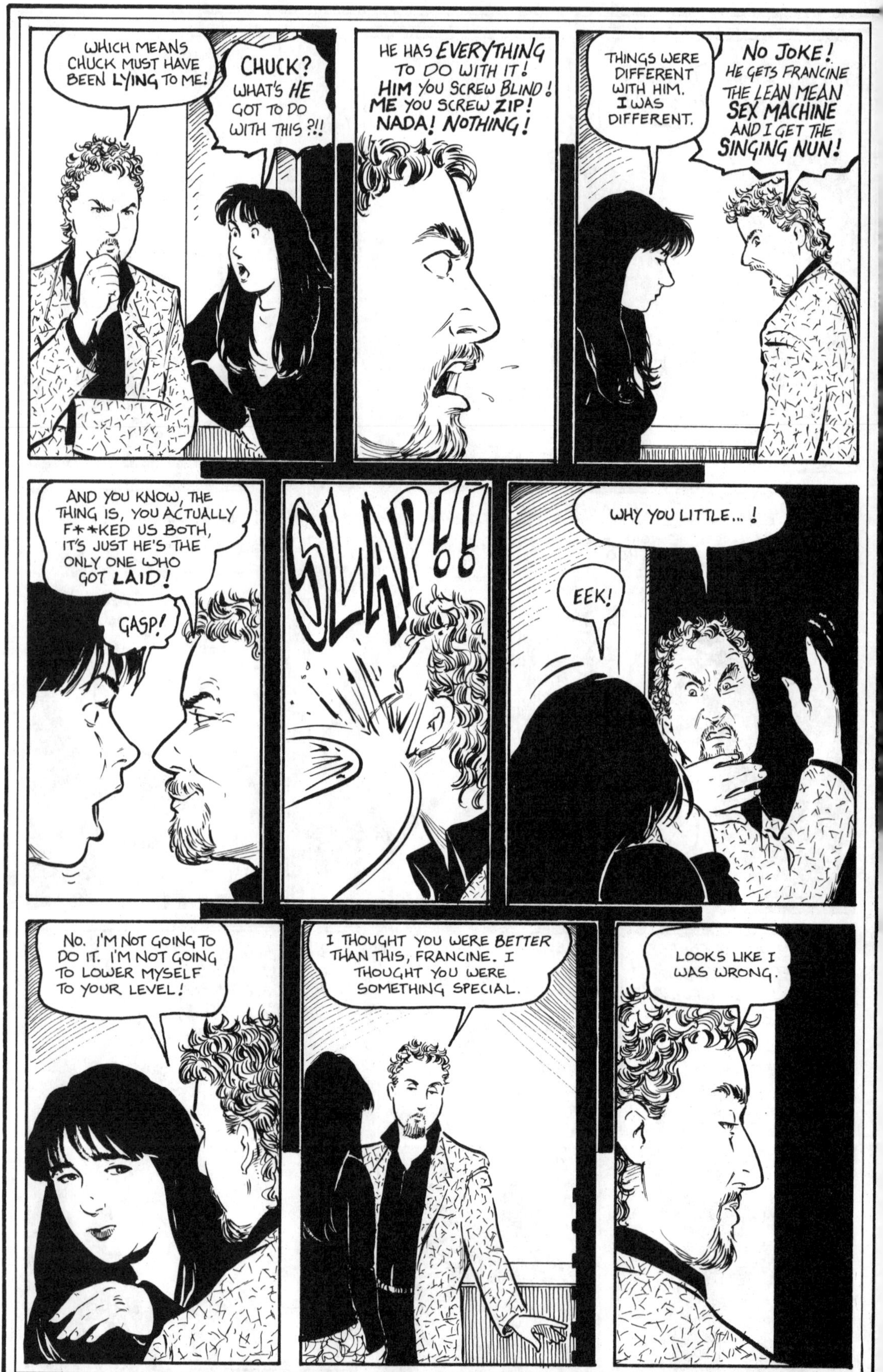
WHICH MEANS CHUCK MUST HAVE BEEN LYING TO ME!
CHUCK? WHAT'S HE GOT TO DO WITH THIS ?!!
HE HAS EVERYTHING TO DO WITH IT! HIM YOU SCREW BLIND! ME YOU SCREW ZIP! NADA! NOTHING!
THINGS WERE DIFFERENT WITH HIM. I WAS DIFFERENT.
NO JOKE! HE GETS FRANCINE THE LEAN MEAN SEX MACHINE AND I GET THE SINGING NUN!
AND YOU KNOW, THE THING IS, YOU ACTUALLY F**KED US BOTH, IT'S JUST HE'S THE ONLY ONE WHO GOT LAID!
GASP!
SLAP!!
WHY YOU LITTLE...!
EEK!
NO. I'M NOT GOING TO DO IT. I'M NOT GOING TO LOWER MYSELF TO YOUR LEVEL!
I THOUGHT YOU WERE BETTER THAN THIS, FRANCINE. I THOUGHT YOU WERE SOMETHING SPECIAL.
LOOKS LIKE I WAS WRONG.

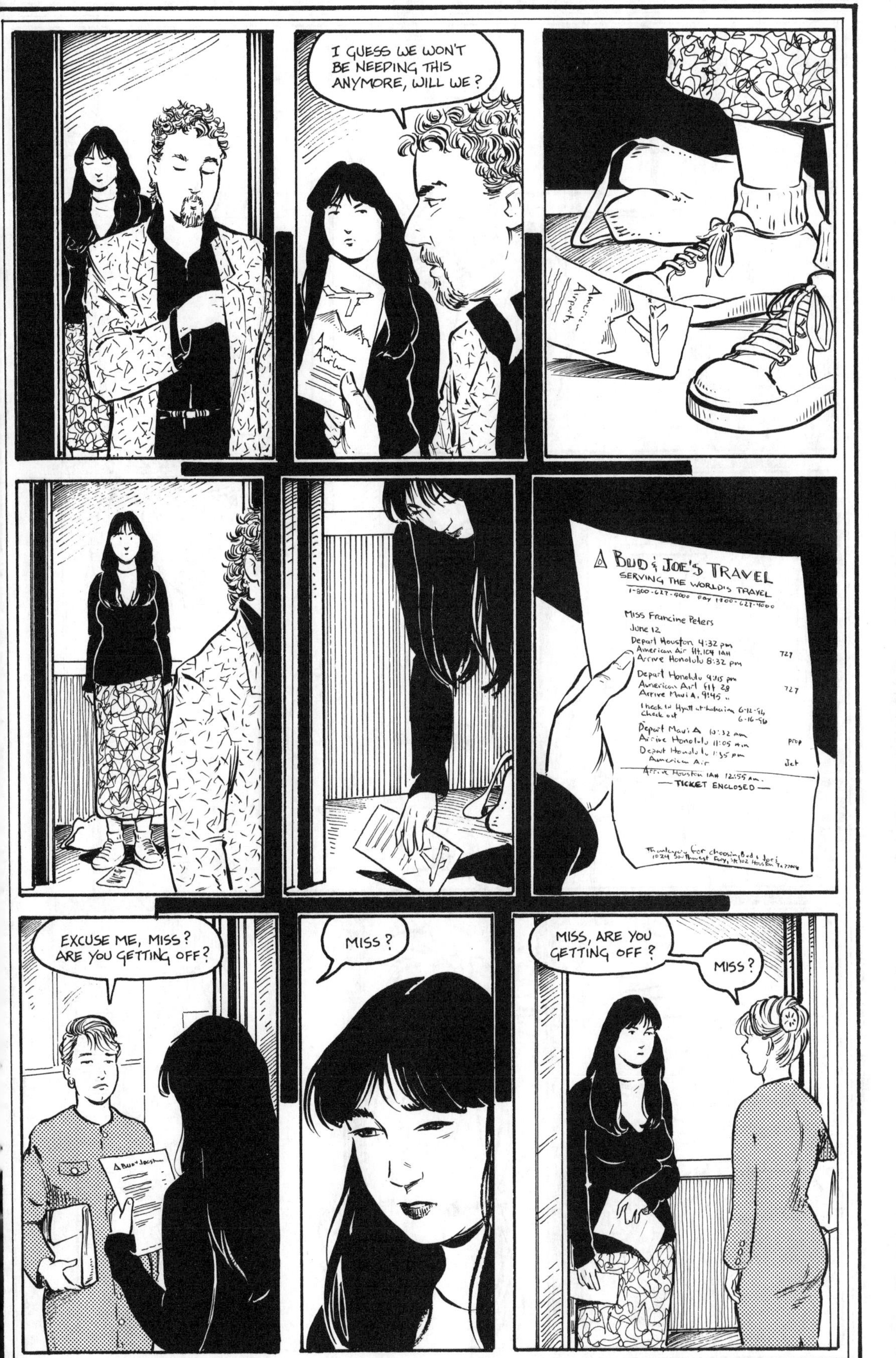
I GUESS WE WON'T BE NEEDING THIS ANYMORE, WILL WE?
BUD & JOE'S TRAVEL
SERVING THE WORLD'S TRAVEL
1-800-627-9000 Fax 1-800-627-4000
Miss Francine Peters
June 12
Depart Houston 4:32 pm
American Air flt. 104 IAH 727
Arrive Honolulu 8:32 pm
Depart Honolulu 9:15 pm
American Air flt 28 727
Arrive Maui A. 9:45
Check in Hyatt at Lahaina 6-12-96
Check out 6-16-96
Depart Maui A 10:32 am
Arrive Honolulu 11:05 a.m. prop
Depart Honolulu 1:35 pm
American Air Jet
Arrive Houston IAH 12:55 am.
— TICKET ENCLOSED —
EXCUSE ME, MISS? ARE YOU GETTING OFF?
MISS?
MISS, ARE YOU GETTING OFF?
MISS?

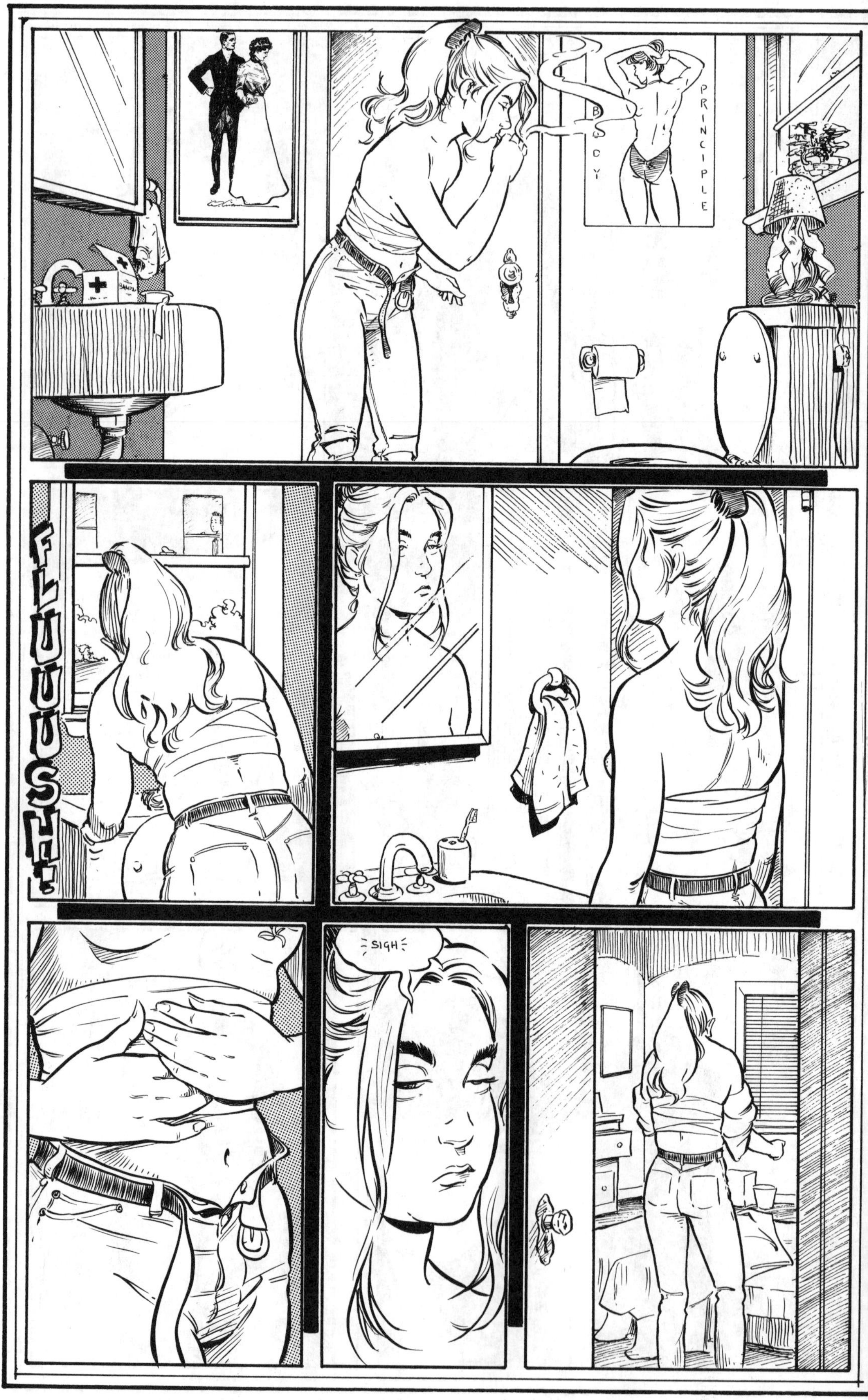
BODY PRINCIPLE
FLUUUUSH!
SIGH

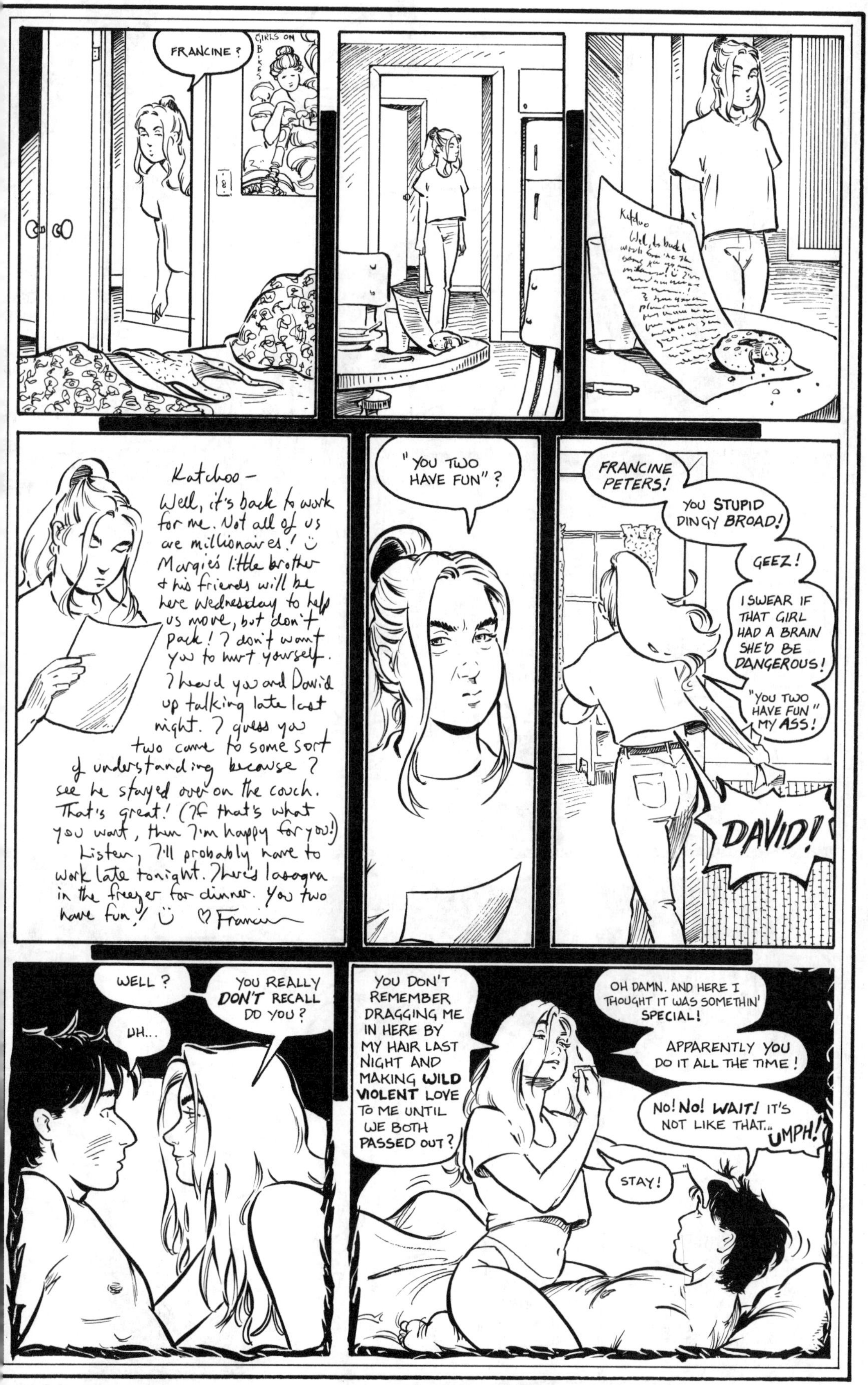
FRANCINE?
GIRLS ON BIKES
Katchoo—
Well, it's back to work for me. Not all of us are millionaires! ☺ Margie's little brother & his friends will be here Wednesday to help us move, but don't pack! I don't want you to hurt yourself.
I heard you and David up talking late last night. I guess you two came to some sort of understanding because I see he stayed over on the couch. That's great! (If that's what you want, then I'm happy for you!)
Listen, I'll probably have to work late tonight. There's lasagna in the freezer for dinner. You two have fun! ☺ ♡ Francine
"YOU TWO HAVE FUN"?
FRANCINE PETERS!
YOU STUPID DINGY BROAD!
GEEZ!
I SWEAR IF THAT GIRL HAD A BRAIN SHE'D BE DANGEROUS!
"YOU TWO HAVE FUN" MY ASS!
DAVID!
WELL?
UH...
YOU REALLY DON'T RECALL DO YOU?
YOU DON'T REMEMBER DRAGGING ME IN HERE BY MY HAIR LAST NIGHT AND MAKING WILD VIOLENT LOVE TO ME UNTIL WE BOTH PASSED OUT?
OH DAMN. AND HERE I THOUGHT IT WAS SOMETHIN' SPECIAL!
APPARENTLY YOU DO IT ALL THE TIME!
NO! NO! WAIT! IT'S NOT LIKE THAT... UMPH!
STAY!

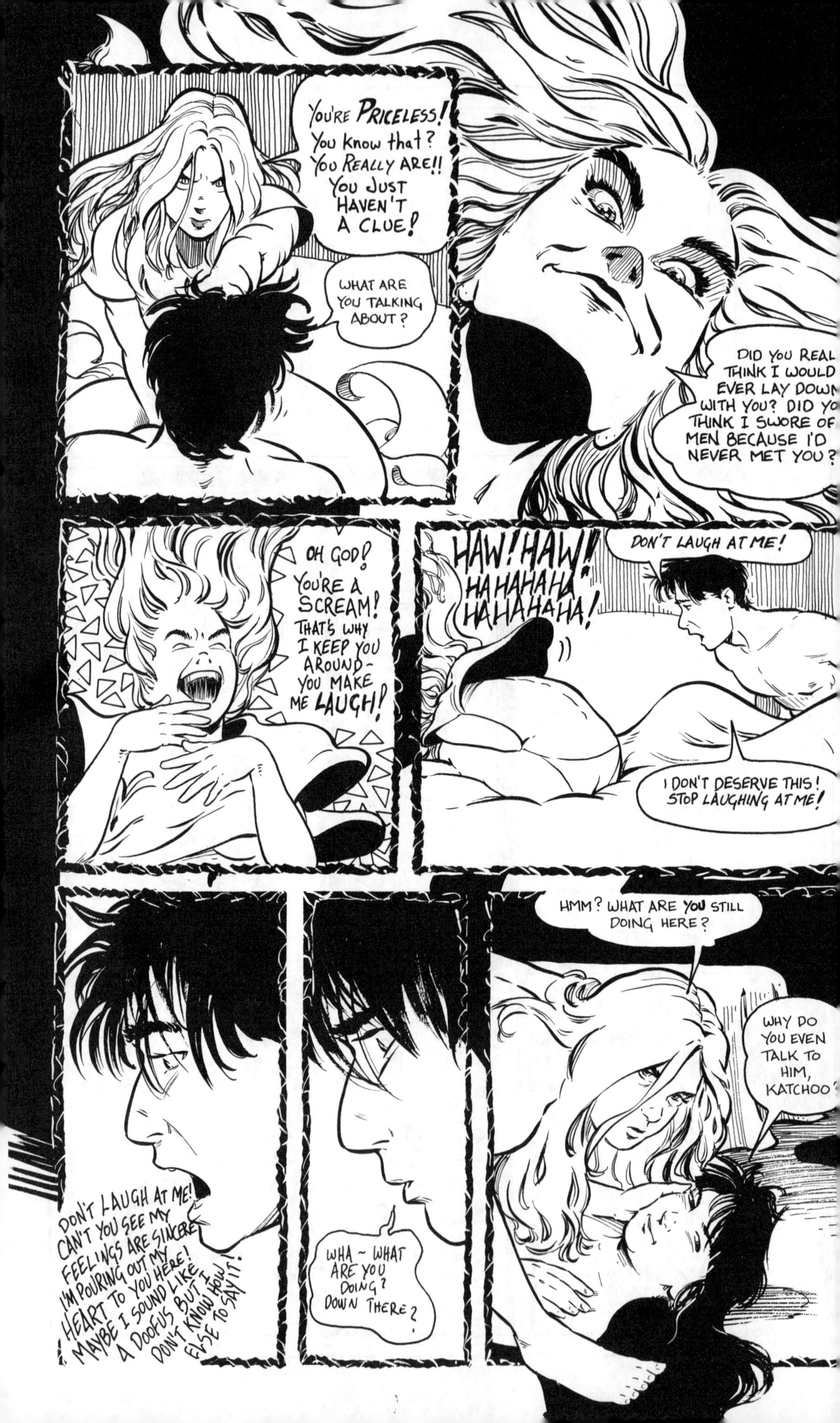

You're PRICELESS! You know that? You REALLY ARE!! You JUST HAVEN'T A CLUE!
WHAT ARE YOU TALKING ABOUT?
DID YOU REAL THINK I WOULD EVER LAY DOWN WITH YOU? DID YO THINK I SWORE OF MEN BECAUSE I'D NEVER MET YOU?
OH GOD! You're A SCREAM! THAT'S WHY I KEEP YOU AROUND - YOU MAKE ME LAUGH!
HAW! HAW! HAHAHAHA HAHAHAHA!
DON'T LAUGH AT ME!
I DON'T DESERVE THIS! STOP LAUGHING AT ME!
DON'T LAUGH AT ME! CAN'T YOU SEE MY FEELINGS ARE SINCERE! I'M POURING OUT MY HEART TO YOU HERE! MAYBE I SOUND LIKE A DOOFUS BUT I DON'T KNOW HOW ELSE TO SAY IT!
WHA ~ WHAT ARE YOU DOING? DOWN THERE?
HMM? WHAT ARE YOU STILL DOING HERE?
WHY DO YOU EVEN TALK TO HIM, KATCHOO?

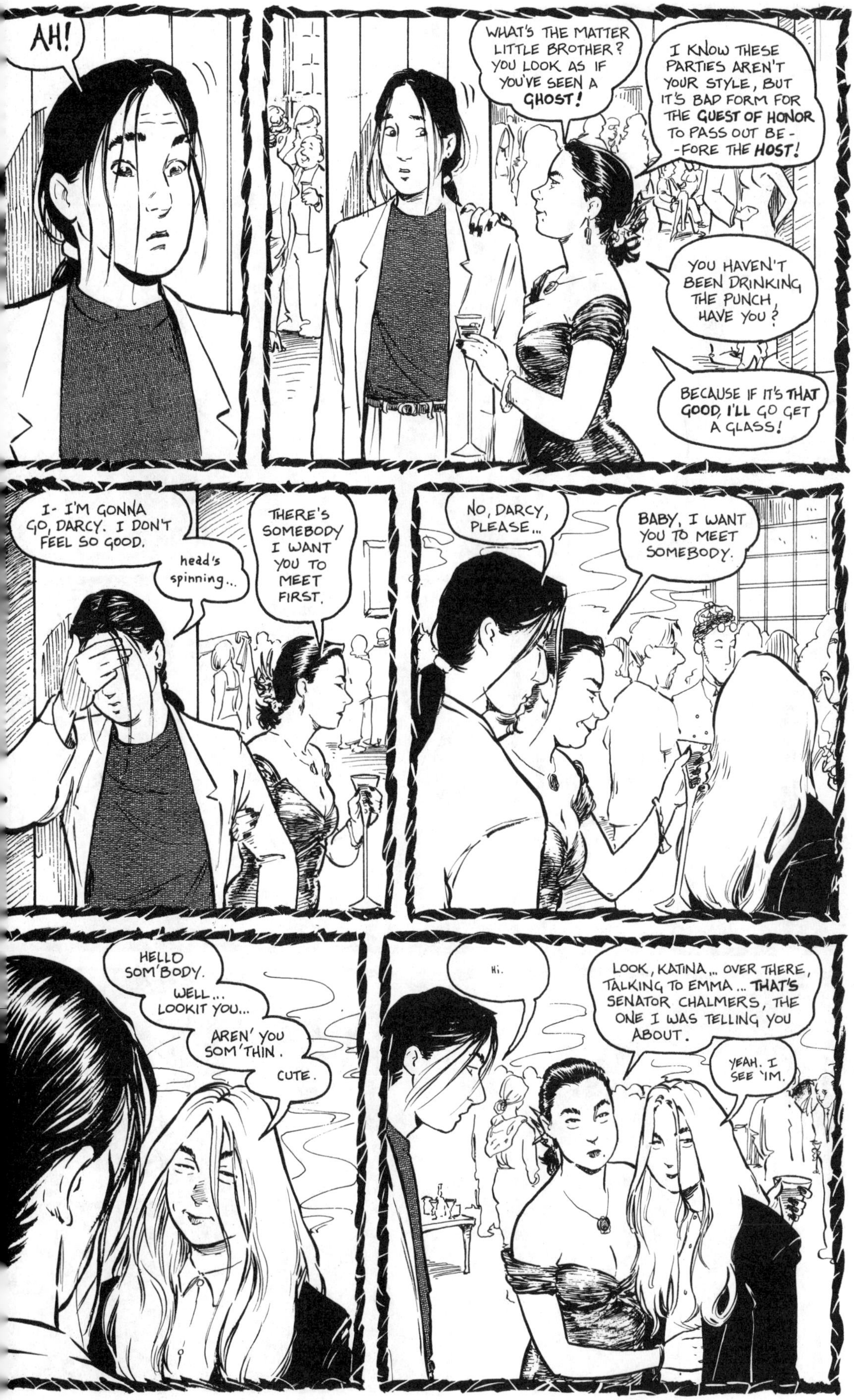

AH!
WHAT'S THE MATTER LITTLE BROTHER? YOU LOOK AS IF YOU'VE SEEN A GHOST!
I KNOW THESE PARTIES AREN'T YOUR STYLE, BUT IT'S BAD FORM FOR THE GUEST OF HONOR TO PASS OUT BE- -FORE THE HOST!
YOU HAVEN'T BEEN DRINKING THE PUNCH, HAVE YOU?
BECAUSE IF IT'S THAT GOOD, I'LL GO GET A GLASS!
I- I'M GONNA GO, DARCY. I DON'T FEEL SO GOOD.
head's spinning...
THERE'S SOMEBODY I WANT YOU TO MEET FIRST.
NO, DARCY, PLEASE...
BABY, I WANT YOU TO MEET SOMEBODY.
HELLO SOM'BODY.
WELL... LOOKIT YOU...
AREN' YOU SOM'THIN.
CUTE.
Hi.
LOOK, KATINA... OVER THERE, TALKING TO EMMA... THAT'S SENATOR CHALMERS, THE ONE I WAS TELLING YOU ABOUT.
YEAH. I SEE 'IM.

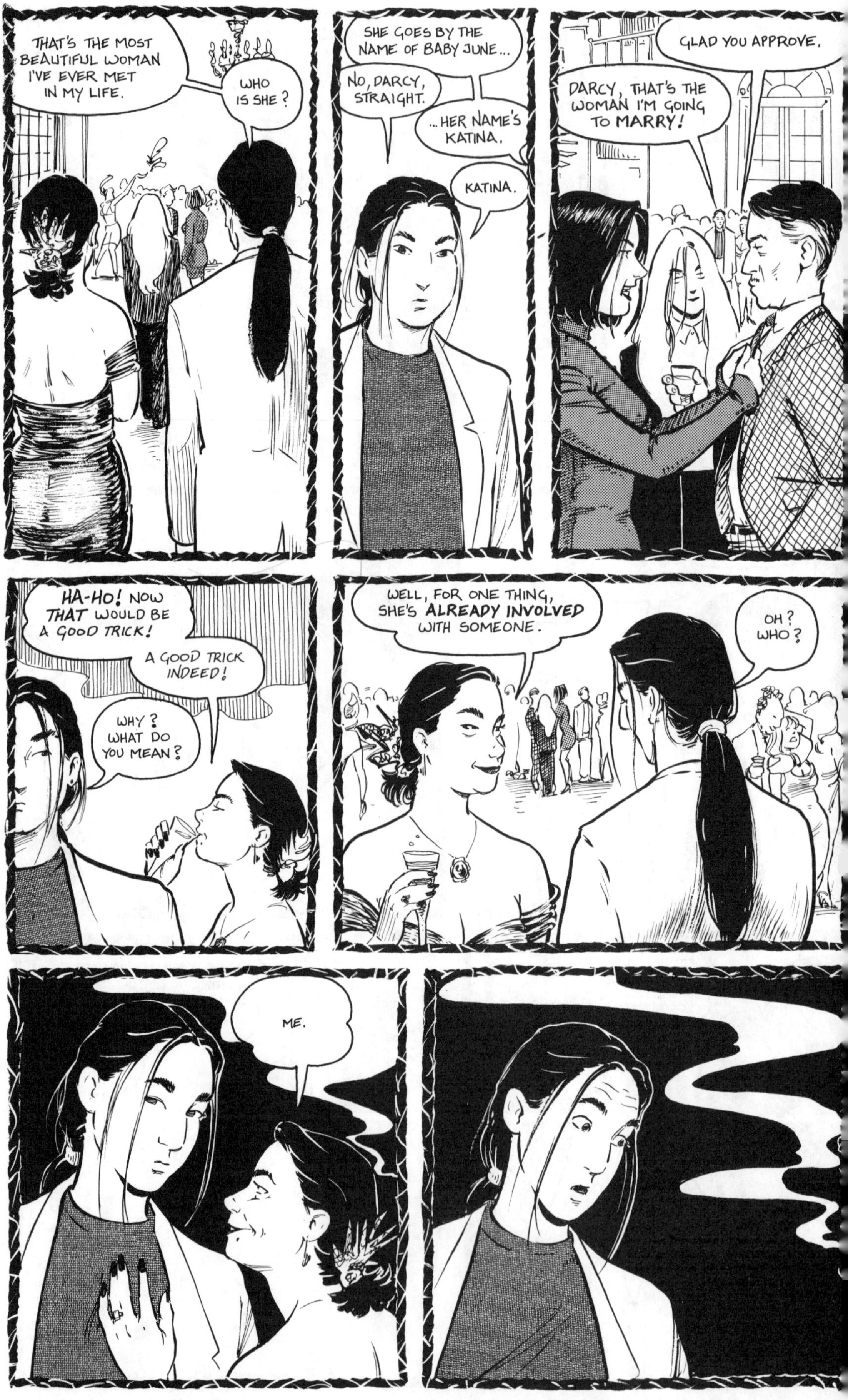
THAT'S THE MOST BEAUTIFUL WOMAN I'VE EVER MET IN MY LIFE.
WHO IS SHE?
SHE GOES BY THE NAME OF BABY JUNE...
NO, DARCY, STRAIGHT.
...HER NAME'S KATINA.
KATINA.
GLAD YOU APPROVE.
DARCY, THAT'S THE WOMAN I'M GOING TO MARRY!
HA-HO! NOW THAT WOULD BE A GOOD TRICK!
A GOOD TRICK INDEED!
WHY? WHAT DO YOU MEAN?
WELL, FOR ONE THING, SHE'S ALREADY INVOLVED WITH SOMEONE.
OH? WHO?
ME.

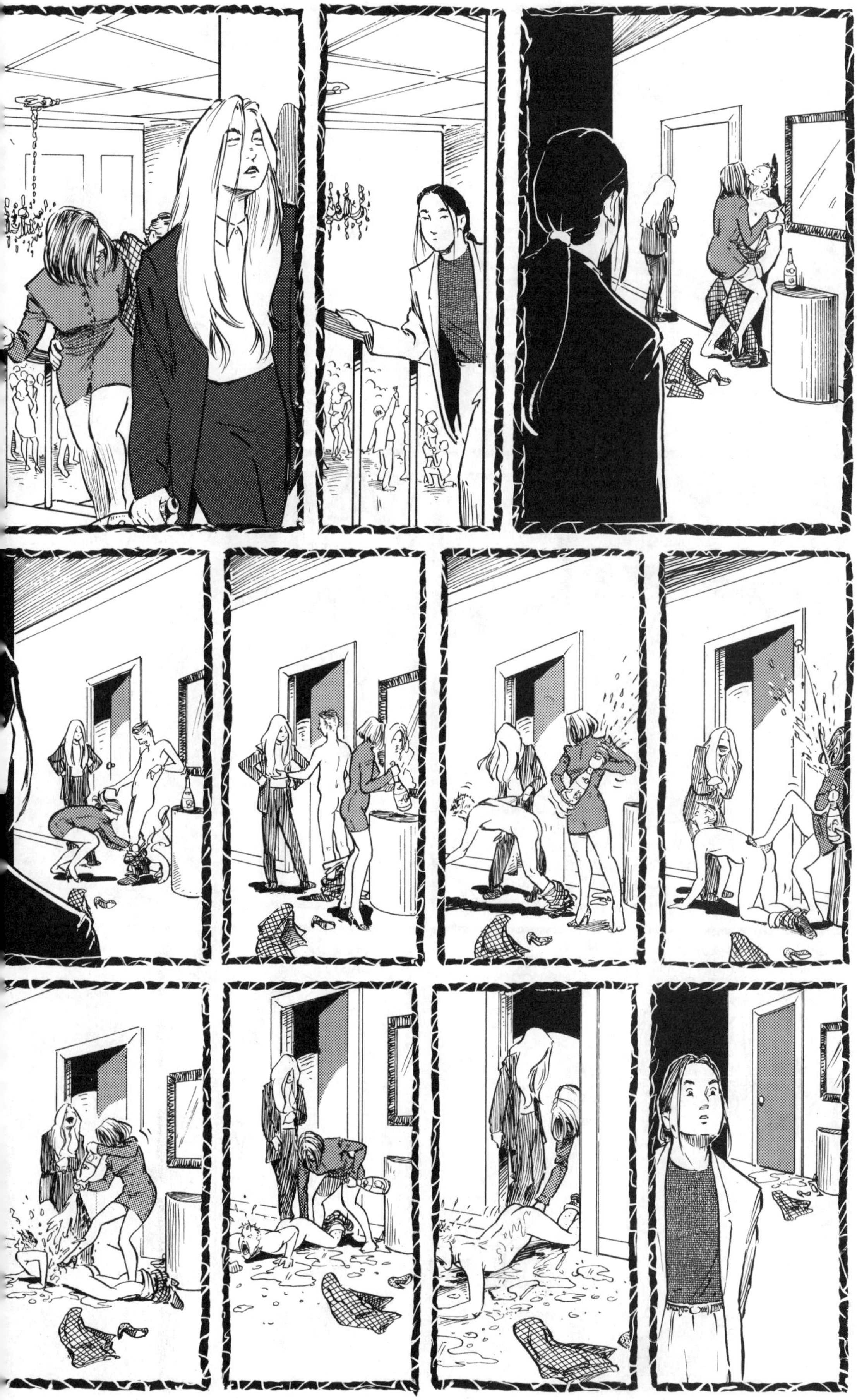

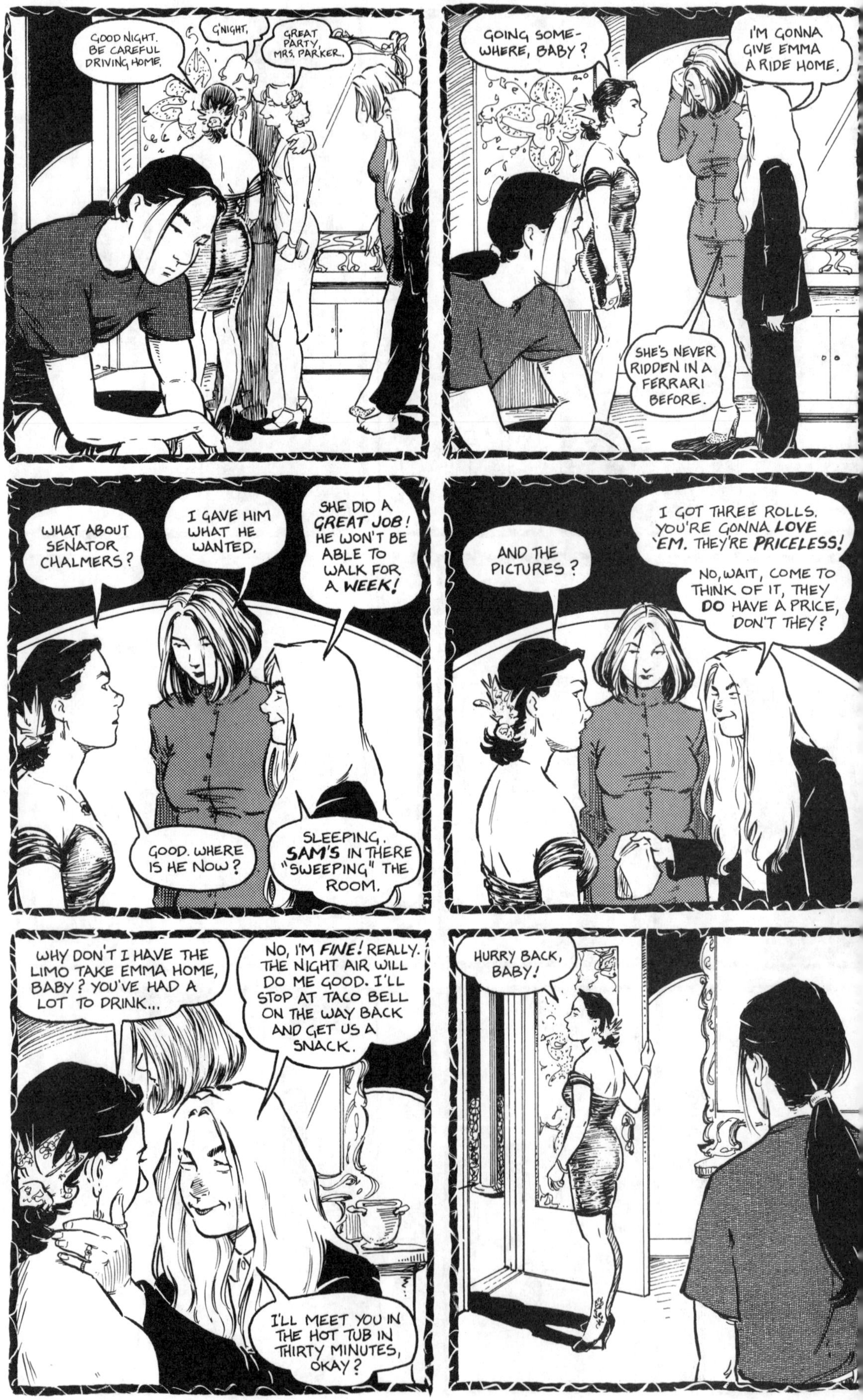
GOOD NIGHT. BE CAREFUL DRIVING HOME.
G'NIGHT,
GREAT PARTY, MRS. PARKER.
GOING SOME-WHERE, BABY?
I'M GONNA GIVE EMMA A RIDE HOME.
SHE'S NEVER RIDDEN IN A FERRARI BEFORE.
WHAT ABOUT SENATOR CHALMERS?
I GAVE HIM WHAT HE WANTED.
SHE DID A GREAT JOB! HE WON'T BE ABLE TO WALK FOR A WEEK!
GOOD. WHERE IS HE NOW?
SLEEPING. SAM'S IN THERE "SWEEPING" THE ROOM.
AND THE PICTURES?
I GOT THREE ROLLS. YOU'RE GONNA LOVE 'EM. THEY'RE PRICELESS!
NO, WAIT, COME TO THINK OF IT, THEY DO HAVE A PRICE, DON'T THEY?
WHY DON'T I HAVE THE LIMO TAKE EMMA HOME, BABY? YOU'VE HAD A LOT TO DRINK...
NO, I'M FINE! REALLY. THE NIGHT AIR WILL DO ME GOOD. I'LL STOP AT TACO BELL ON THE WAY BACK AND GET US A SNACK.
I'LL MEET YOU IN THE HOT TUB IN THIRTY MINUTES, OKAY?
HURRY BACK, BABY!

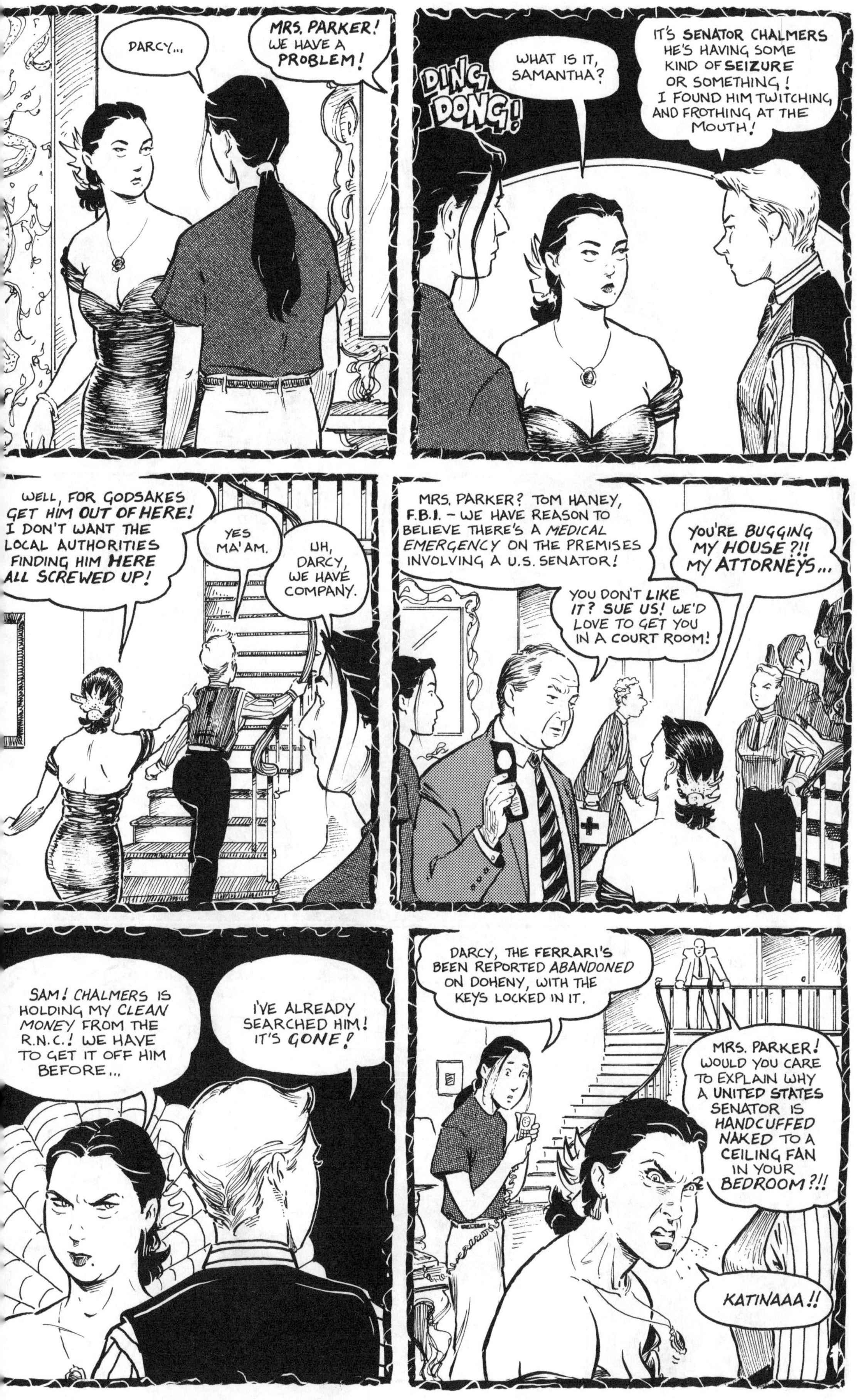
DARCY...
MRS. PARKER! WE HAVE A PROBLEM!
DING DONG!
WHAT IS IT, SAMANTHA?
IT'S SENATOR CHALMERS HE'S HAVING SOME KIND OF SEIZURE OR SOMETHING! I FOUND HIM TWITCHING AND FROTHING AT THE MOUTH!
WELL, FOR GODSAKES GET HIM OUT OF HERE! I DON'T WANT THE LOCAL AUTHORITIES FINDING HIM HERE ALL SCREWED UP!
YES MA'AM.
UH, DARCY, WE HAVE COMPANY.
MRS. PARKER? TOM HANEY, F.B.I. - WE HAVE REASON TO BELIEVE THERE'S A MEDICAL EMERGENCY ON THE PREMISES INVOLVING A U.S. SENATOR!
YOU'RE BUGGING MY HOUSE?!! MY ATTORNEYS...
YOU DON'T LIKE IT? SUE US! WE'D LOVE TO GET YOU IN A COURT ROOM!
SAM! CHALMERS IS HOLDING MY CLEAN MONEY FROM THE R.N.C.! WE HAVE TO GET IT OFF HIM BEFORE...
I'VE ALREADY SEARCHED HIM! IT'S GONE!
DARCY, THE FERRARI'S BEEN REPORTED ABANDONED ON DOHENY, WITH THE KEYS LOCKED IN IT.
MRS. PARKER! WOULD YOU CARE TO EXPLAIN WHY A UNITED STATES SENATOR IS HANDCUFFED NAKED TO A CEILING FAN IN YOUR BEDROOM?!!
KATINAAA!!

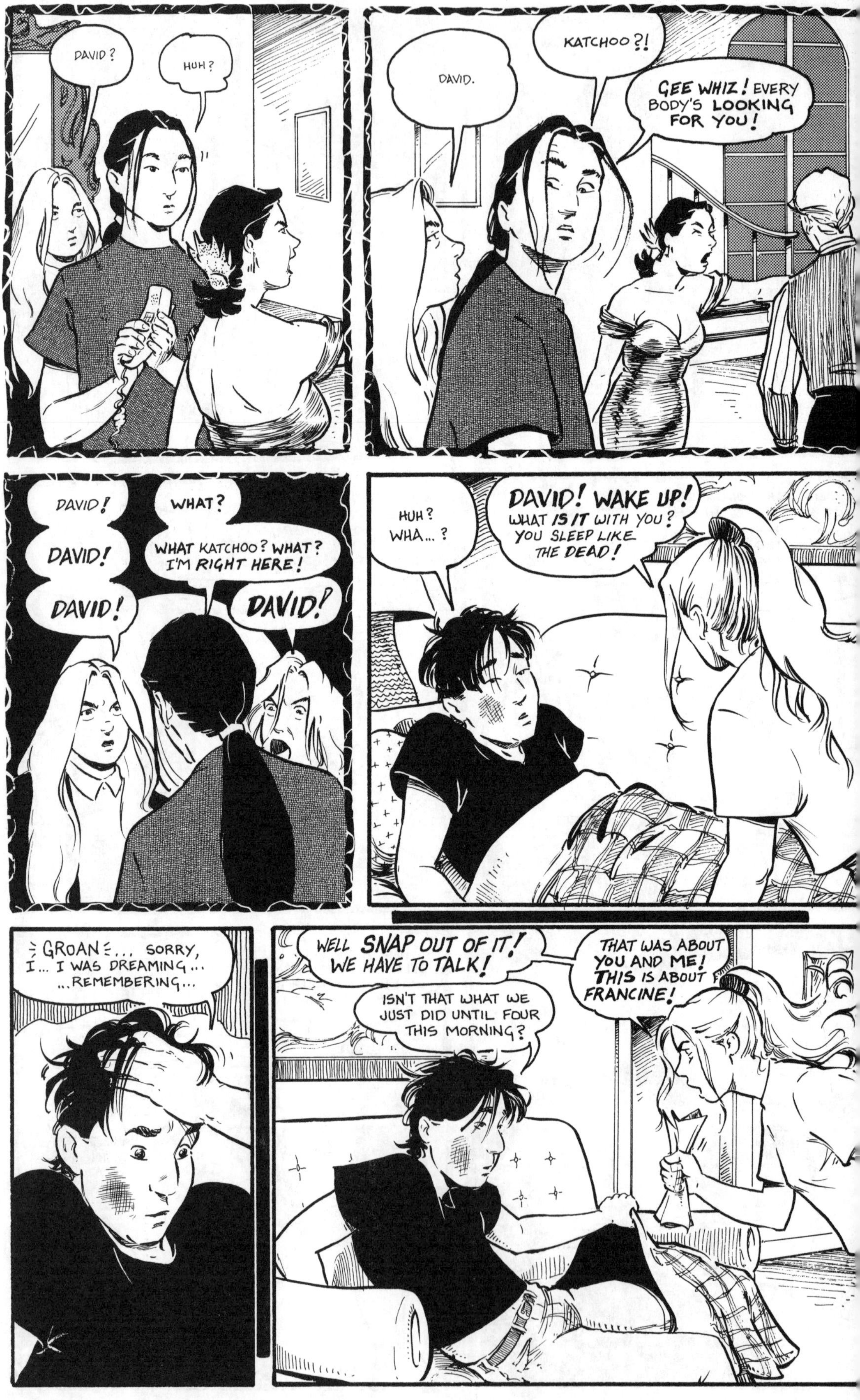
DAVID?
HUH?
DAVID.
KATCHOO?!
GEE WHIZ! EVERY BODY'S LOOKING FOR YOU!
DAVID!
DAVID!
DAVID!
WHAT?
WHAT KATCHOO? WHAT? I'M RIGHT HERE!
DAVID!
HUH? WHA...?
DAVID! WAKE UP! WHAT IS IT WITH YOU? YOU SLEEP LIKE THE DEAD!
GROAN... SORRY, I... I WAS DREAMING... ...REMEMBERING...
WELL SNAP OUT OF IT! WE HAVE TO TALK!
ISN'T THAT WHAT WE JUST DID UNTIL FOUR THIS MORNING?
THAT WAS ABOUT YOU AND ME! THIS IS ABOUT FRANCINE!

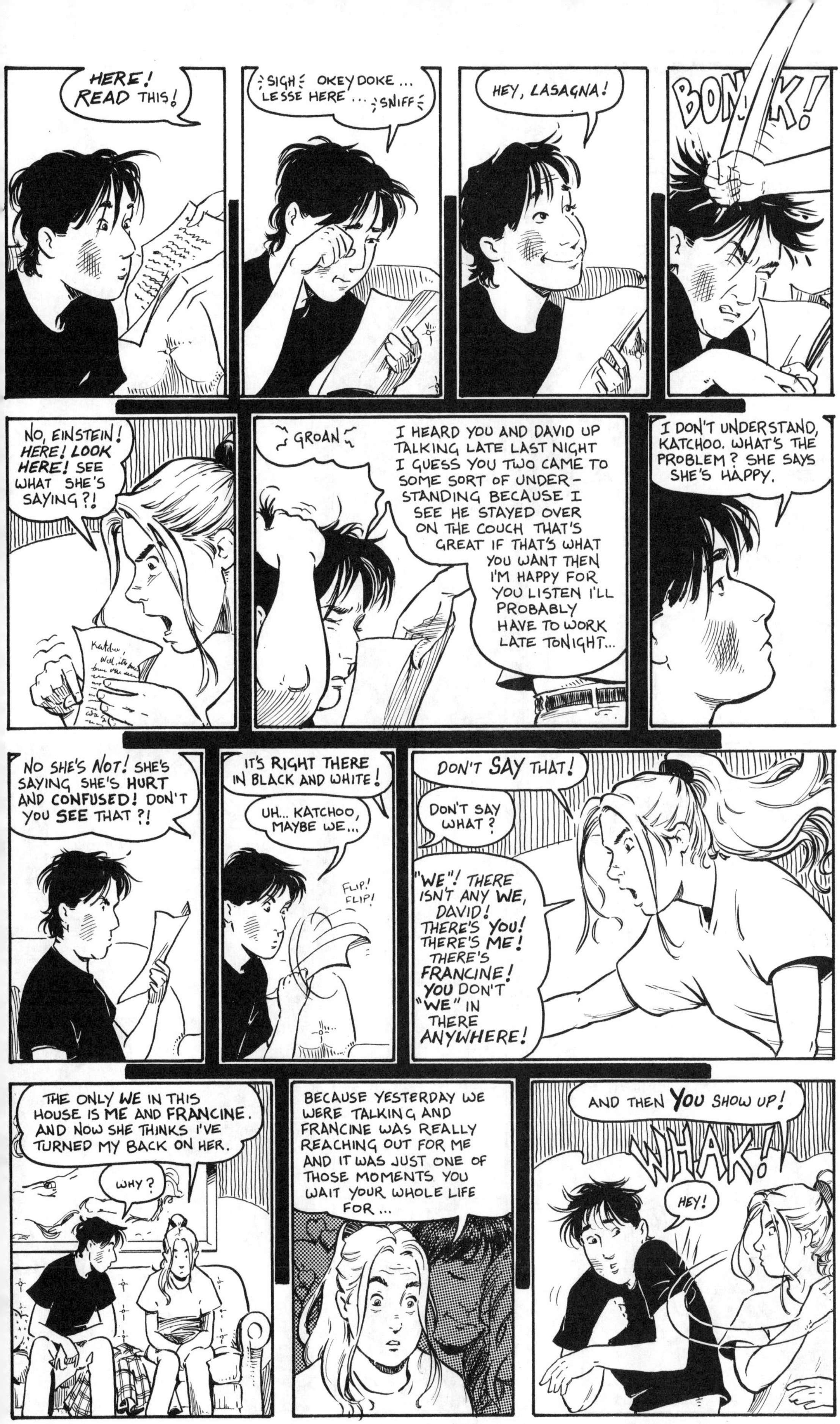
HERE! READ THIS!
SIGH OKEYDOKE... LESSE HERE... SNIFF
HEY, LASAGNA!
BONK!
NO, EINSTEIN! HERE! LOOK HERE! SEE WHAT SHE'S SAYING?!
GROAN
I HEARD YOU AND DAVID UP TALKING LATE LAST NIGHT I GUESS YOU TWO CAME TO SOME SORT OF UNDER-STANDING BECAUSE I SEE HE STAYED OVER ON THE COUCH THAT'S GREAT IF THAT'S WHAT YOU WANT THEN I'M HAPPY FOR YOU LISTEN I'LL PROBABLY HAVE TO WORK LATE TONIGHT...
I DON'T UNDERSTAND, KATCHOO. WHAT'S THE PROBLEM? SHE SAYS SHE'S HAPPY.
NO SHE'S NOT! SHE'S SAYING SHE'S HURT AND CONFUSED! DON'T YOU SEE THAT?!
IT'S RIGHT THERE IN BLACK AND WHITE!
UH... KATCHOO, MAYBE WE...
FLIP! FLIP!
DON'T SAY THAT!
DON'T SAY WHAT?
"WE"! THERE ISN'T ANY WE, DAVID! THERE'S YOU! THERE'S ME! THERE'S FRANCINE! YOU DON'T "WE" IN THERE ANYWHERE!
THE ONLY WE IN THIS HOUSE IS ME AND FRANCINE. AND NOW SHE THINKS I'VE TURNED MY BACK ON HER.
WHY?
BECAUSE YESTERDAY WE WERE TALKING AND FRANCINE WAS REALLY REACHING OUT FOR ME AND IT WAS JUST ONE OF THOSE MOMENTS YOU WAIT YOUR WHOLE LIFE FOR...
AND THEN YOU SHOW UP!
WHAK!
HEY!

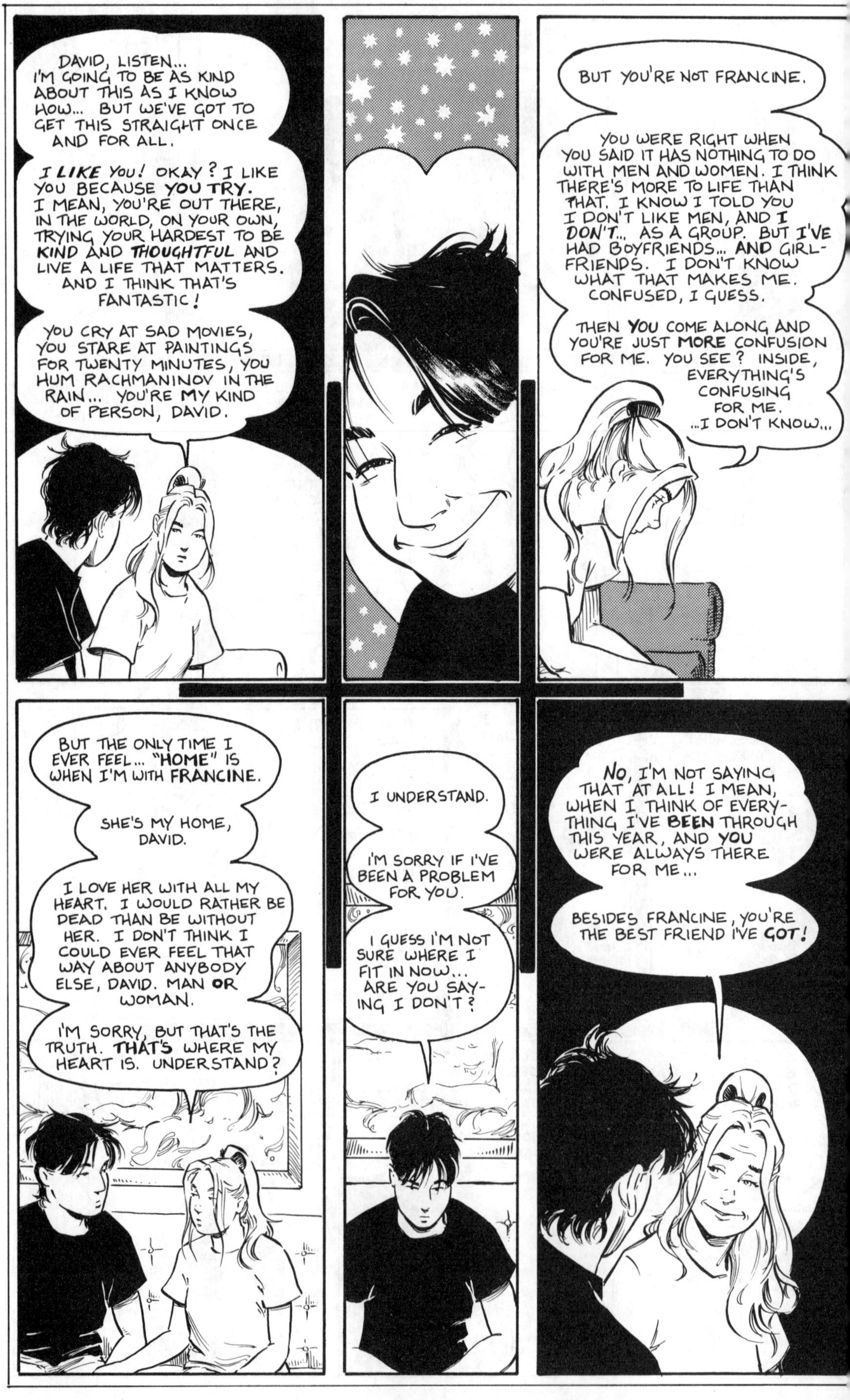
DAVID, LISTEN... I'M GOING TO BE AS KIND ABOUT THIS AS I KNOW HOW... BUT WE'VE GOT TO GET THIS STRAIGHT ONCE AND FOR ALL.
I LIKE YOU! OKAY? I LIKE YOU BECAUSE YOU TRY. I MEAN, YOU'RE OUT THERE, IN THE WORLD, ON YOUR OWN, TRYING YOUR HARDEST TO BE KIND AND THOUGHTFUL AND LIVE A LIFE THAT MATTERS. AND I THINK THAT'S FANTASTIC!
YOU CRY AT SAD MOVIES, YOU STARE AT PAINTINGS FOR TWENTY MINUTES, YOU HUM RACHMANINOV IN THE RAIN... YOU'RE MY KIND OF PERSON, DAVID.
BUT YOU'RE NOT FRANCINE.
YOU WERE RIGHT WHEN YOU SAID IT HAS NOTHING TO DO WITH MEN AND WOMEN. I THINK THERE'S MORE TO LIFE THAN THAT. I KNOW I TOLD YOU I DON'T LIKE MEN, AND I DON'T... AS A GROUP. BUT I'VE HAD BOYFRIENDS... AND GIRLFRIENDS. I DON'T KNOW WHAT THAT MAKES ME. CONFUSED, I GUESS.
THEN YOU COME ALONG AND YOU'RE JUST MORE CONFUSION FOR ME. YOU SEE? INSIDE, EVERYTHING'S CONFUSING FOR ME. ...I DON'T KNOW...
BUT THE ONLY TIME I EVER FEEL... "HOME" IS WHEN I'M WITH FRANCINE.
SHE'S MY HOME, DAVID.
I LOVE HER WITH ALL MY HEART. I WOULD RATHER BE DEAD THAN BE WITHOUT HER. I DON'T THINK I COULD EVER FEEL THAT WAY ABOUT ANYBODY ELSE, DAVID. MAN OR WOMAN.
I'M SORRY, BUT THAT'S THE TRUTH. THAT'S WHERE MY HEART IS. UNDERSTAND?
I UNDERSTAND.
I'M SORRY IF I'VE BEEN A PROBLEM FOR YOU.
I GUESS I'M NOT SURE WHERE I FIT IN NOW... ARE YOU SAYING I DON'T?
NO, I'M NOT SAYING THAT AT ALL! I MEAN, WHEN I THINK OF EVERYTHING I'VE BEEN THROUGH THIS YEAR, AND YOU WERE ALWAYS THERE FOR ME...
BESIDES FRANCINE, YOU'RE THE BEST FRIEND I'VE GOT!

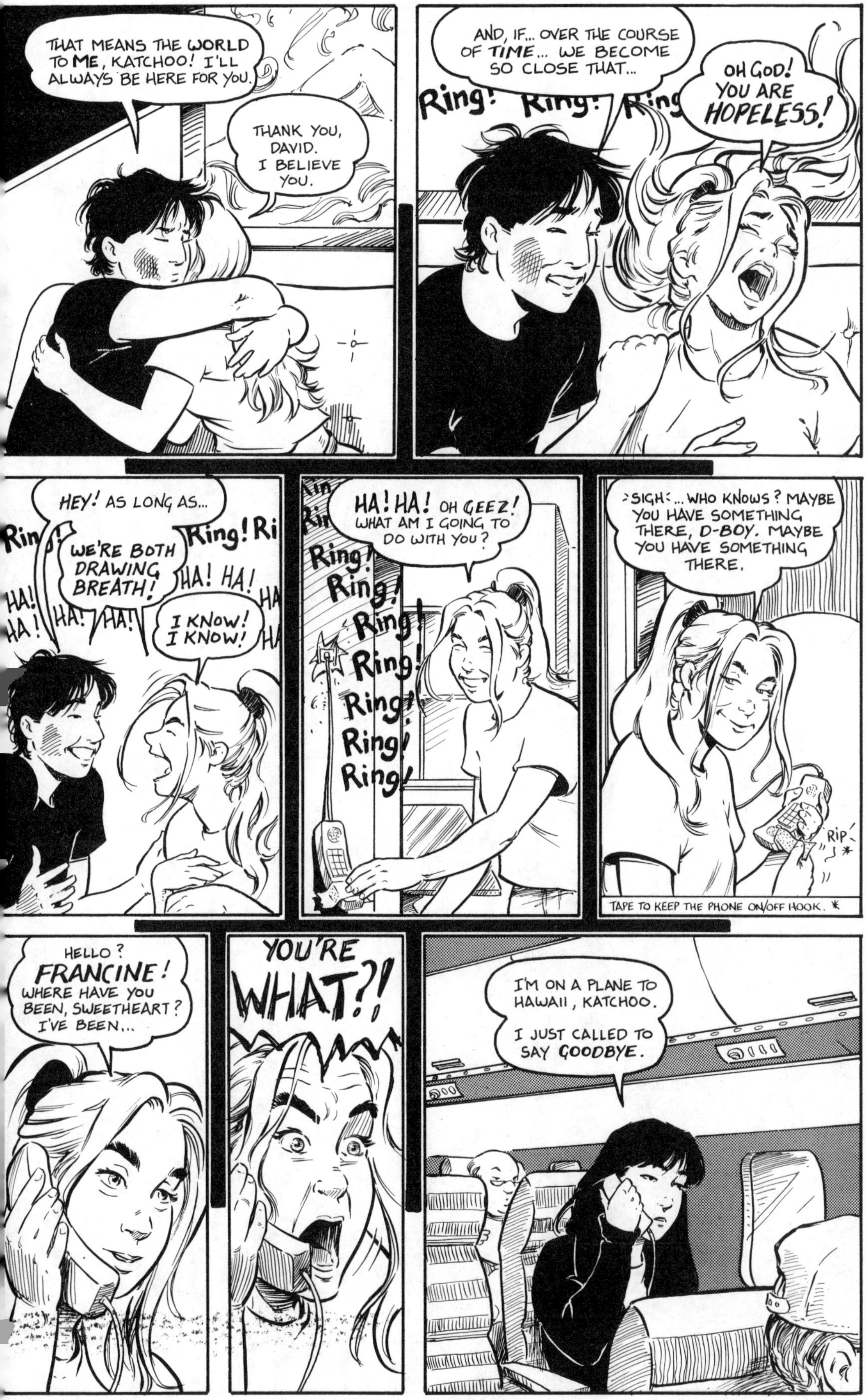

THAT MEANS THE WORLD TO ME, KATCHOO! I'LL ALWAYS BE HERE FOR YOU.
THANK YOU, DAVID. I BELIEVE YOU.
AND, IF... OVER THE COURSE OF TIME... WE BECOME SO CLOSE THAT...
Ring! Ring! Ring
OH GOD! YOU ARE HOPELESS!
HEY! AS LONG AS...
WE'RE BOTH DRAWING BREATH!
Ring! Ring! Ri
HA! HA! HA! HA! HA! HA!
I KNOW! I KNOW!
HA! HA! OH GEEZ! WHAT AM I GOING TO DO WITH YOU?
Ring! Ring! Ring! Ring! Ring! Ring! Ring!
>SIGH< ... WHO KNOWS? MAYBE YOU HAVE SOMETHING THERE, D-BOY. MAYBE YOU HAVE SOMETHING THERE.
RIP!
TAPE TO KEEP THE PHONE ON/OFF HOOK. *
HELLO? FRANCINE! WHERE HAVE YOU BEEN, SWEETHEART? I'VE BEEN...
YOU'RE WHAT?!
I'M ON A PLANE TO HAWAII, KATCHOO.
I JUST CALLED TO SAY GOODBYE.

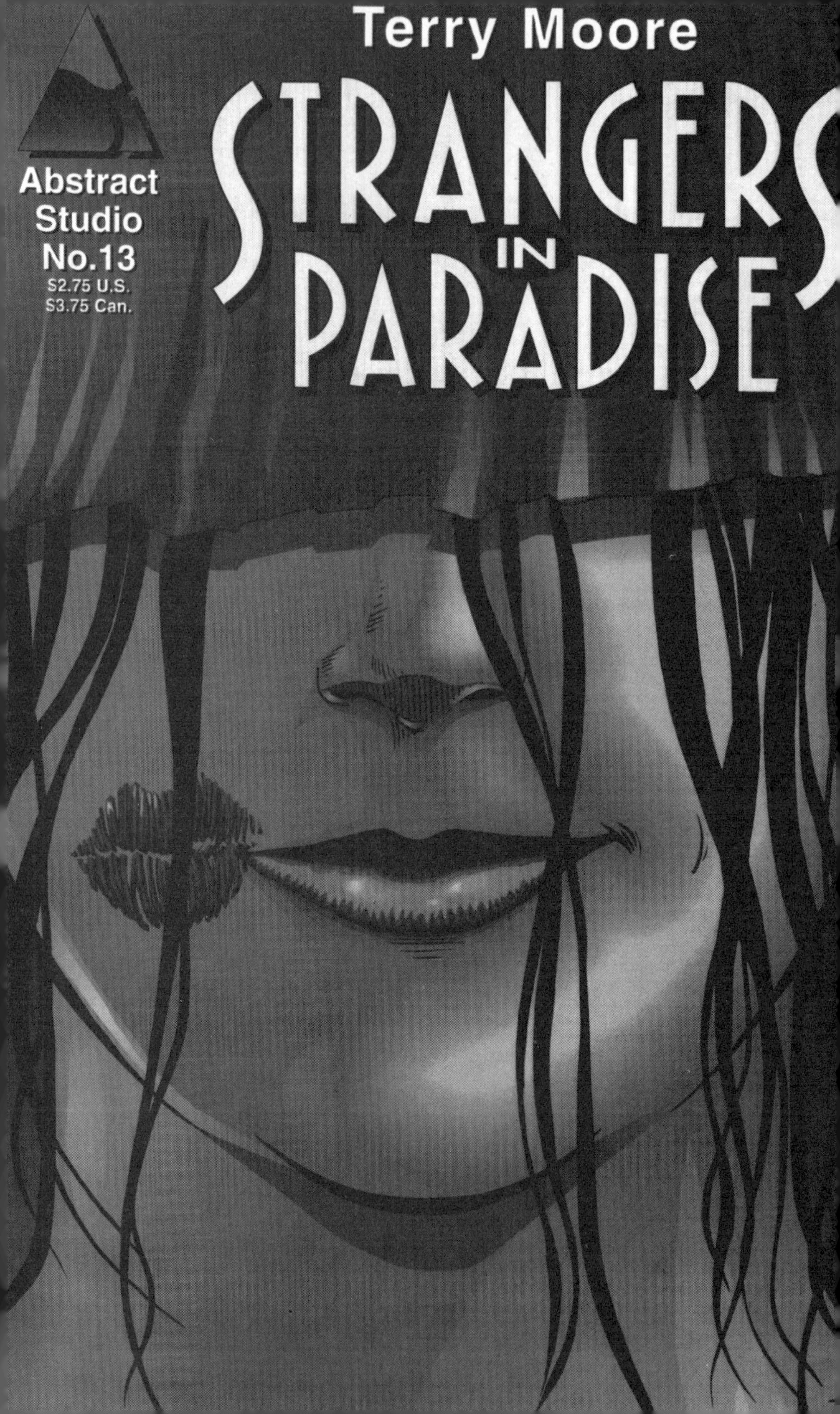

Terry Moore
STRANGERS IN PARADISE
Abstract Studio
No.13
$2.75 U.S.
$3.75 Can.

All of my life
I was waiting for you
How is it we never met?
Here in the latter days
Time on my own
I find too much to regret.
All of the time I spend
Thinking of you
Nothing to say but I call.
Over and Over

It plays on my mind
How come you come and you go?
How is it happening only to me?
Now after all of the time we spent
I was careless and made a slip
Suddenly your love is
Too much to lose

Now I've fallen in love with you.
Were you waiting for
My heart to break?
Though I've fallen
In love with you
I have fallen in love
Too late.

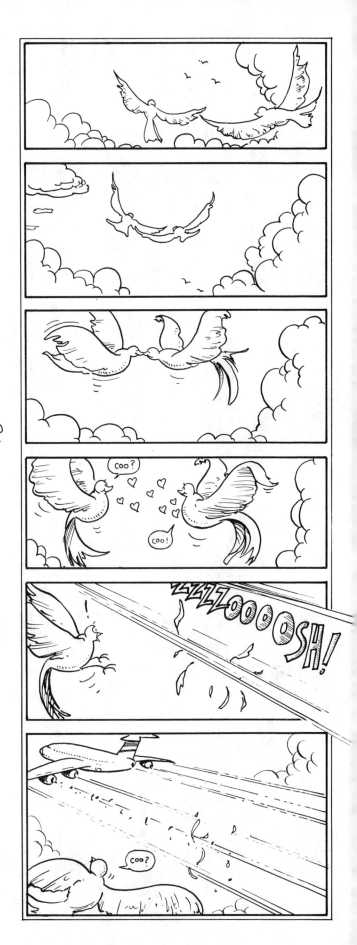

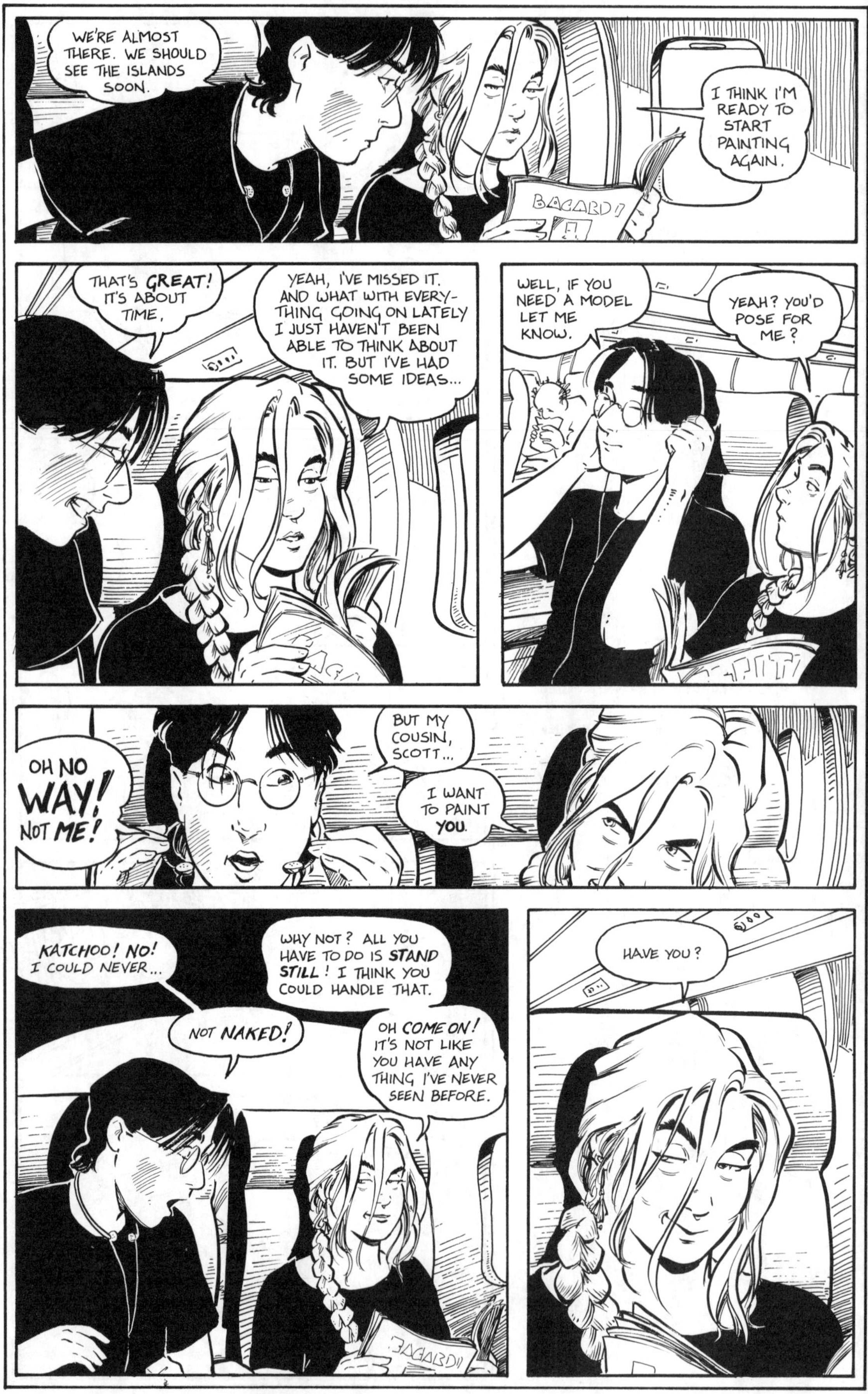
WE'RE ALMOST THERE. WE SHOULD SEE THE ISLANDS SOON.
I THINK I'M READY TO START PAINTING AGAIN.
BAGARDI
THAT'S GREAT! IT'S ABOUT TIME.
YEAH, I'VE MISSED IT. AND WHAT WITH EVERY-THING GOING ON LATELY I JUST HAVEN'T BEEN ABLE TO THINK ABOUT IT. BUT I'VE HAD SOME IDEAS...
WELL, IF YOU NEED A MODEL LET ME KNOW.
YEAH? YOU'D POSE FOR ME?
OH NO WAY! NOT ME!
BUT MY COUSIN, SCOTT...
I WANT TO PAINT YOU.
KATCHOO! NO! I COULD NEVER...
NOT NAKED!
WHY NOT? ALL YOU HAVE TO DO IS STAND STILL! I THINK YOU COULD HANDLE THAT.
OH COME ON! IT'S NOT LIKE YOU HAVE ANY THING I'VE NEVER SEEN BEFORE.
HAVE YOU?

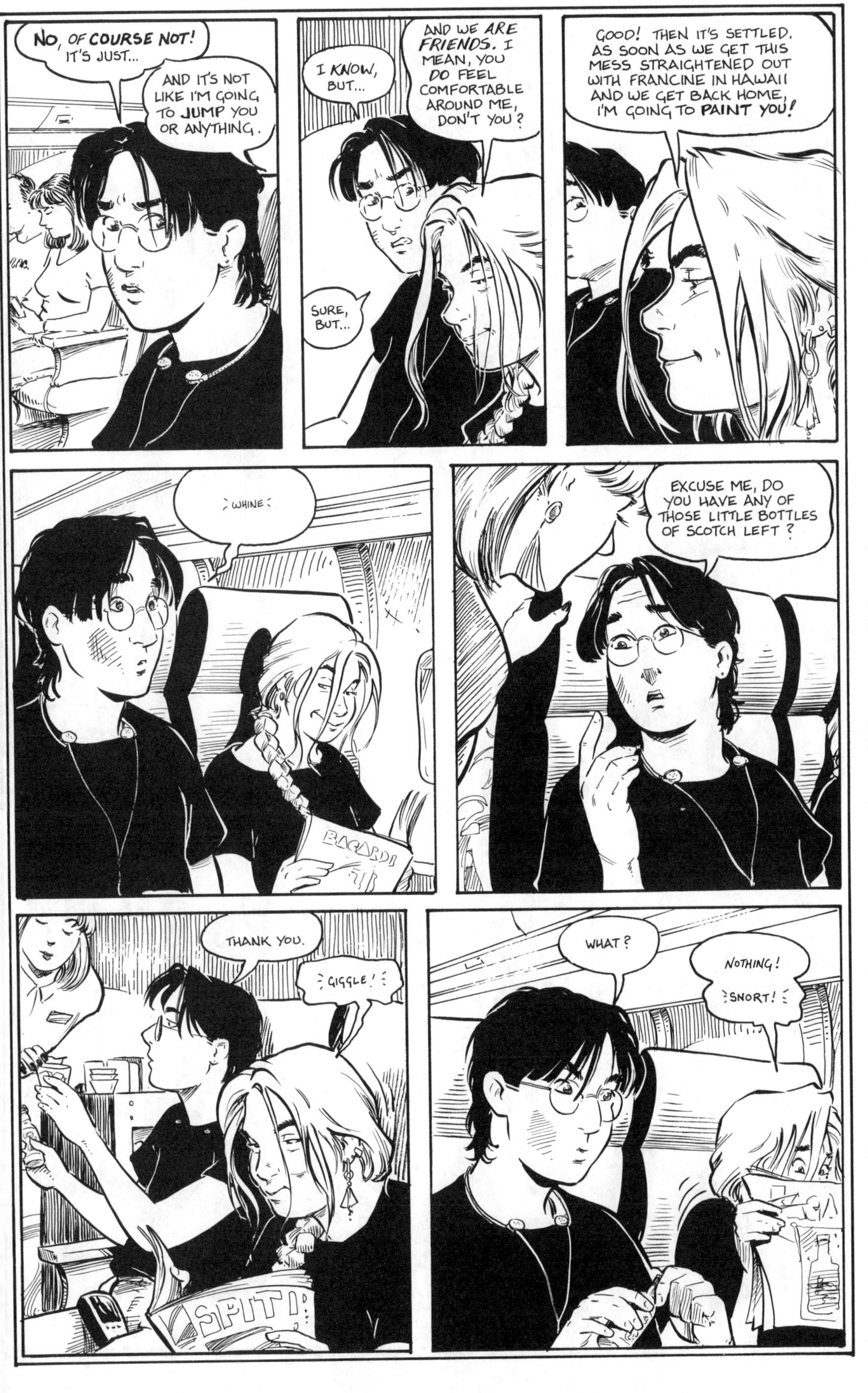
NO, OF COURSE NOT! IT'S JUST...
AND IT'S NOT LIKE I'M GOING TO JUMP YOU OR ANYTHING.
I KNOW, BUT...
AND WE ARE FRIENDS. I MEAN, YOU DO FEEL COMFORTABLE AROUND ME, DON'T YOU?
SURE, BUT...
GOOD! THEN IT'S SETTLED. AS SOON AS WE GET THIS MESS STRAIGHTENED OUT WITH FRANCINE IN HAWAII AND WE GET BACK HOME, I'M GOING TO PAINT YOU!
WHINE
BACARDI
EXCUSE ME, DO YOU HAVE ANY OF THOSE LITTLE BOTTLES OF SCOTCH LEFT?
THANK YOU.
GIGGLE!
SPIT!
WHAT?
NOTHING!
SNORT!

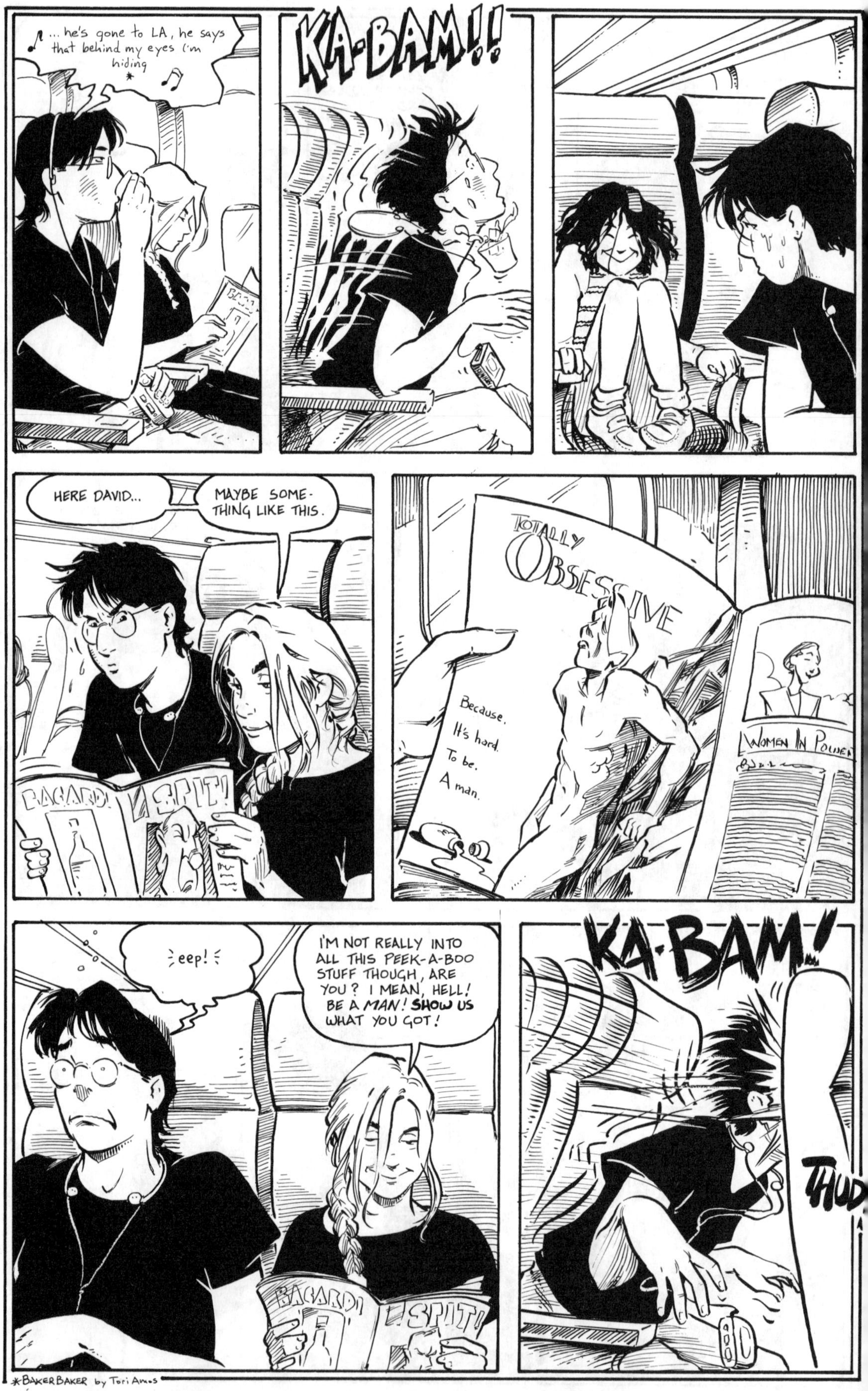

... he's gone to LA, he says that behind my eyes i'm hiding *
KA-BAM!!
HERE DAVID...
MAYBE SOMETHING LIKE THIS.
TOTALLY OBSSESSIVE
Because. It's hard. To be. A man.
WOMEN IN POWER
BACARDI
SPIT!
eep!
I'M NOT REALLY INTO ALL THIS PEEK-A-BOO STUFF THOUGH, ARE YOU? I MEAN, HELL! BE A MAN! SHOW US WHAT YOU GOT!
BACARDI
SPIT!
KA-BAM!
THUD

*BAKERBAKER by Tori Amos

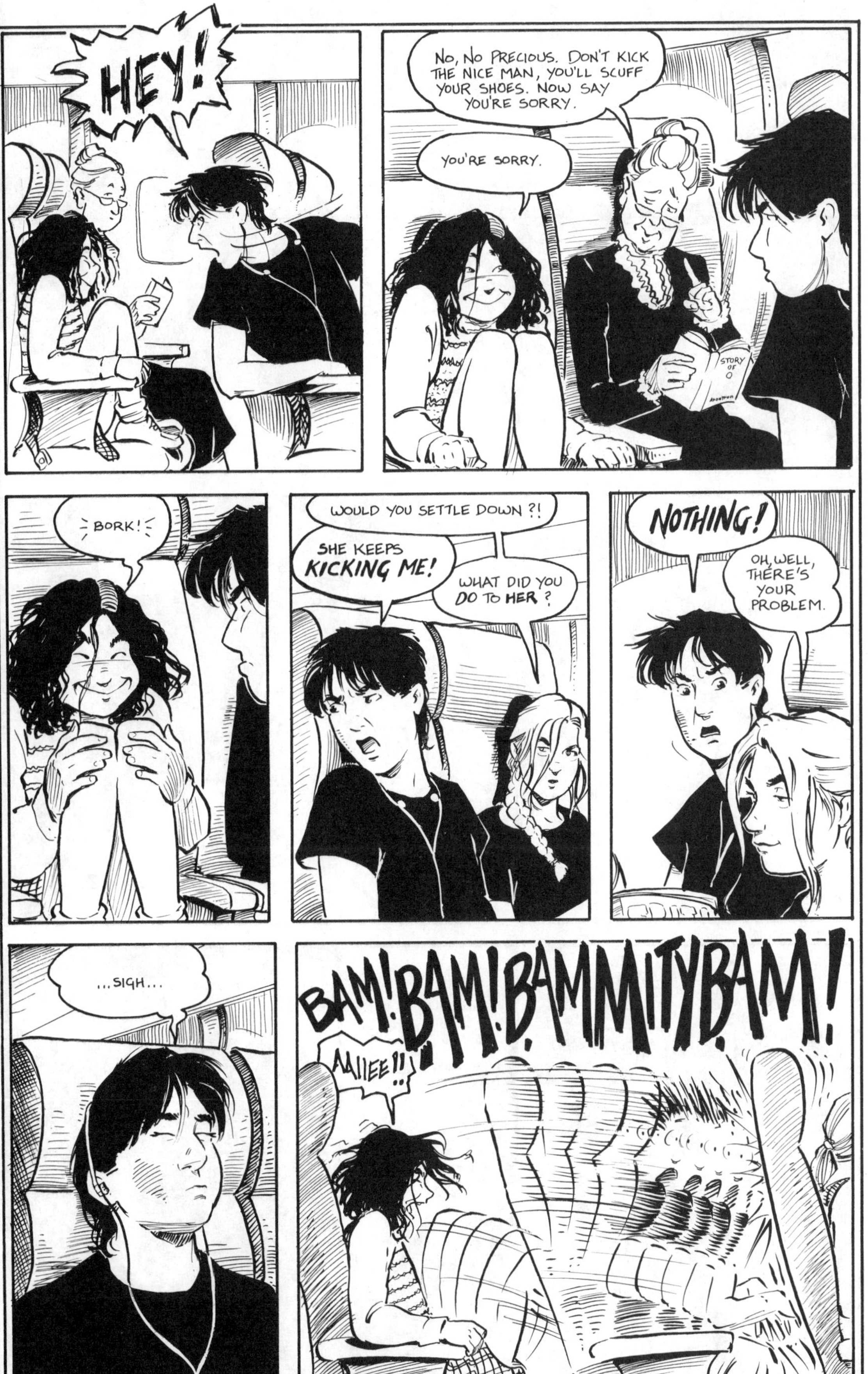
HEY!
NO, NO PRECIOUS. DON'T KICK THE NICE MAN, YOU'LL SCUFF YOUR SHOES. NOW SAY YOU'RE SORRY.
YOU'RE SORRY.
STORY OF O
BORK!
WOULD YOU SETTLE DOWN ?!
SHE KEEPS KICKING ME!
WHAT DID YOU DO TO HER ?
NOTHING!
OH, WELL, THERE'S YOUR PROBLEM.
...SIGH...
BAM! BAM! BAMMITYBAM!
AAIIEE!!

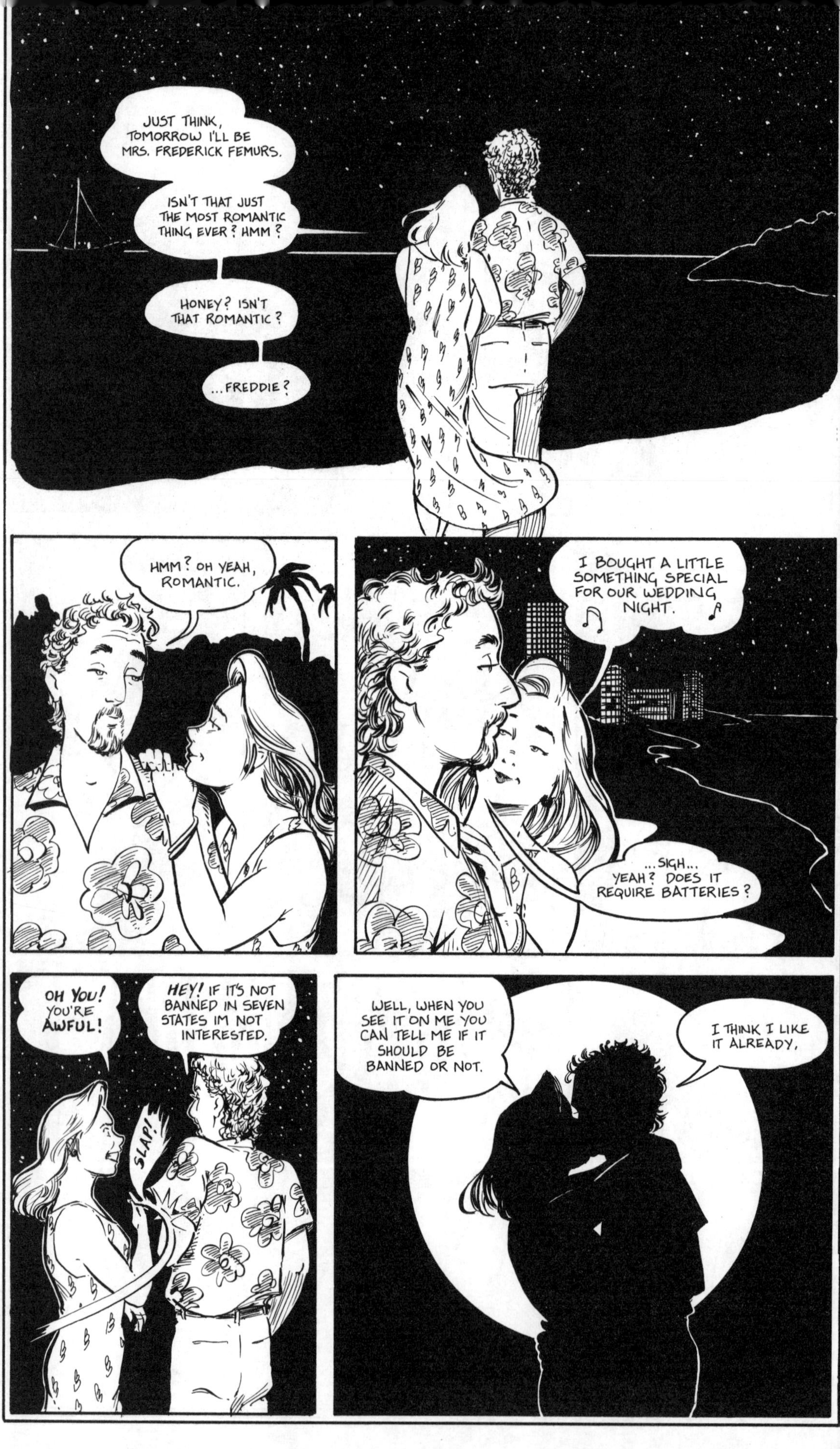
JUST THINK, TOMORROW I'LL BE MRS. FREDERICK FEMURS.
ISN'T THAT JUST THE MOST ROMANTIC THING EVER? HMM?
HONEY? ISN'T THAT ROMANTIC?
...FREDDIE?
HMM? OH YEAH, ROMANTIC.
I BOUGHT A LITTLE SOMETHING SPECIAL FOR OUR WEDDING NIGHT.
...SIGH... YEAH? DOES IT REQUIRE BATTERIES?
OH YOU! YOU'RE AWFUL!
HEY! IF IT'S NOT BANNED IN SEVEN STATES IM NOT INTERESTED.
SLAP!
WELL, WHEN YOU SEE IT ON ME YOU CAN TELL ME IF IT SHOULD BE BANNED OR NOT.
I THINK I LIKE IT ALREADY.

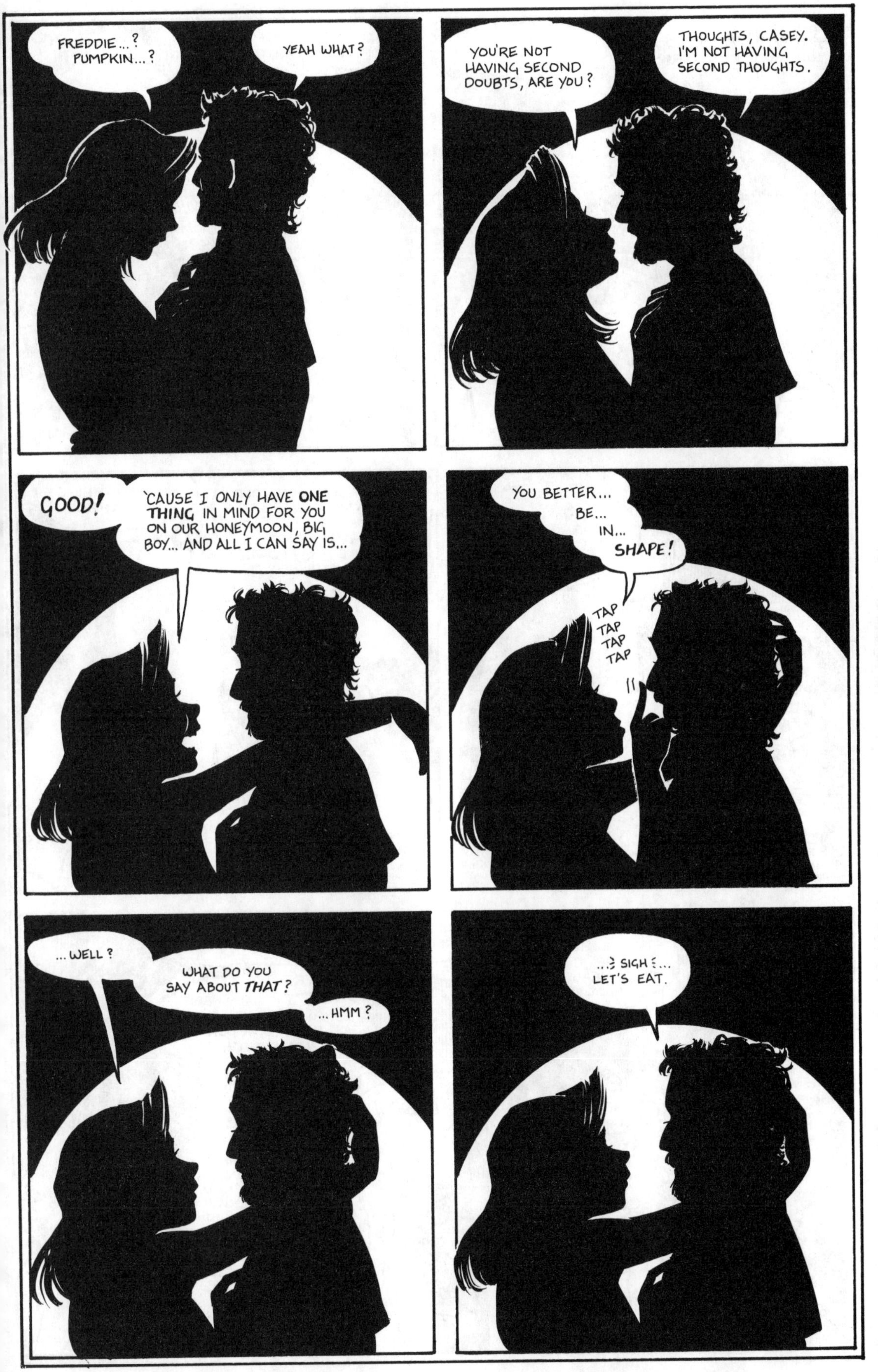
FREDDIE...? PUMPKIN...?
YEAH WHAT?
YOU'RE NOT HAVING SECOND DOUBTS, ARE YOU?
THOUGHTS, CASEY. I'M NOT HAVING SECOND THOUGHTS.
GOOD!
'CAUSE I ONLY HAVE ONE THING IN MIND FOR YOU ON OUR HONEYMOON, BIG BOY... AND ALL I CAN SAY IS...
YOU BETTER... BE... IN... SHAPE!
TAP TAP TAP TAP
...WELL?
WHAT DO YOU SAY ABOUT THAT?
...HMM?
...{ SIGH }... LET'S EAT.

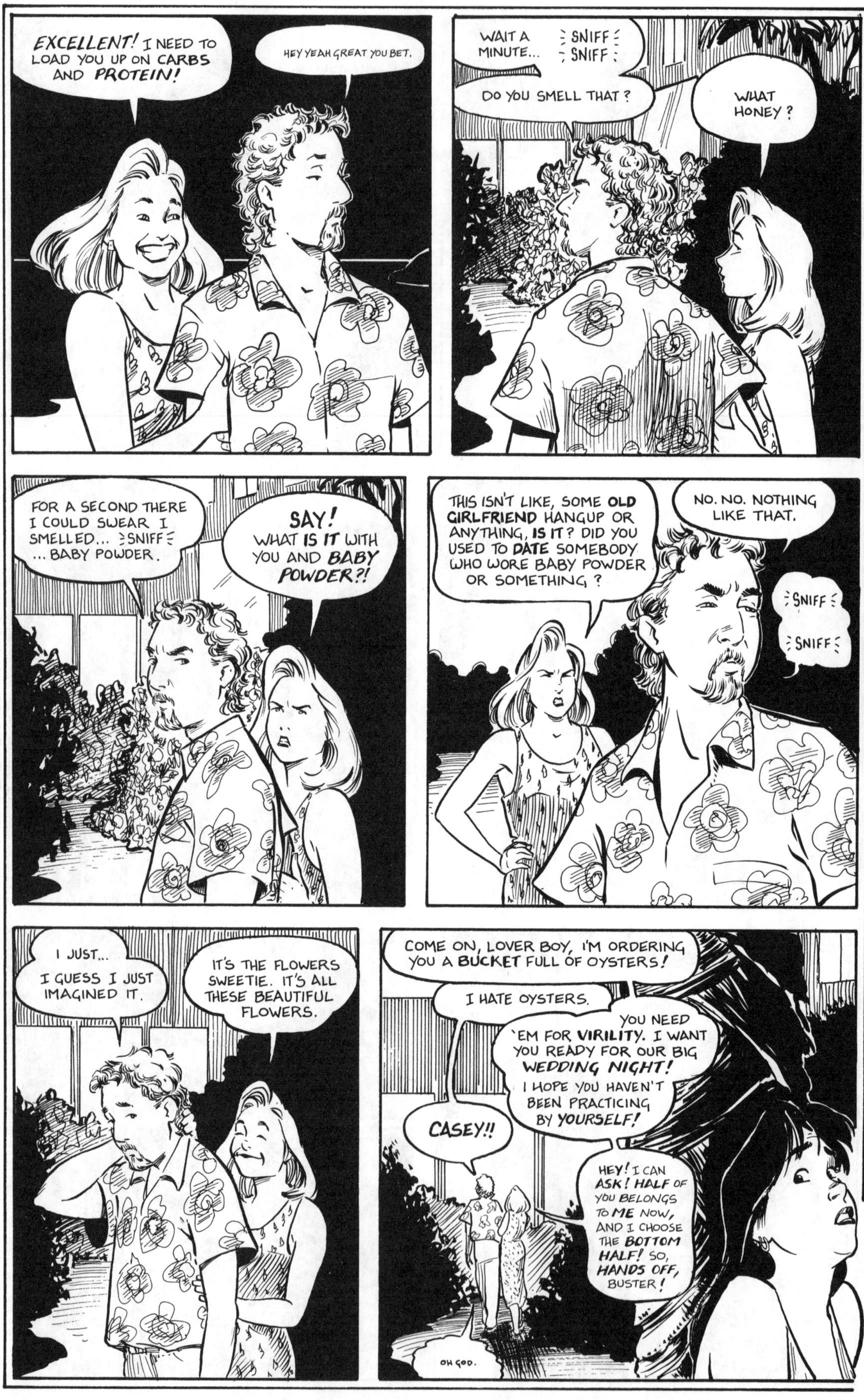
EXCELLENT! I NEED TO LOAD YOU UP ON CARBS AND PROTEIN!
HEY YEAH GREAT YOU BET.
WAIT A MINUTE... SNIFF SNIFF
DO YOU SMELL THAT?
WHAT HONEY?
FOR A SECOND THERE I COULD SWEAR I SMELLED... SNIFF ... BABY POWDER.
SAY! WHAT IS IT WITH YOU AND BABY POWDER?!
THIS ISN'T LIKE, SOME OLD GIRLFRIEND HANGUP OR ANYTHING, IS IT? DID YOU USED TO DATE SOMEBODY WHO WORE BABY POWDER OR SOMETHING?
NO. NO. NOTHING LIKE THAT.
SNIFF
SNIFF
I JUST...
I GUESS I JUST IMAGINED IT.
IT'S THE FLOWERS SWEETIE. IT'S ALL THESE BEAUTIFUL FLOWERS.
COME ON, LOVER BOY, I'M ORDERING YOU A BUCKET FULL OF OYSTERS!
I HATE OYSTERS.
YOU NEED `EM FOR VIRILITY. I WANT YOU READY FOR OUR BIG WEDDING NIGHT!
I HOPE YOU HAVEN'T BEEN PRACTICING BY YOURSELF!
CASEY!!
HEY! I CAN ASK! HALF OF YOU BELONGS TO ME NOW, AND I CHOOSE THE BOTTOM HALF! SO, HANDS OFF, BUSTER!
OH GOD.

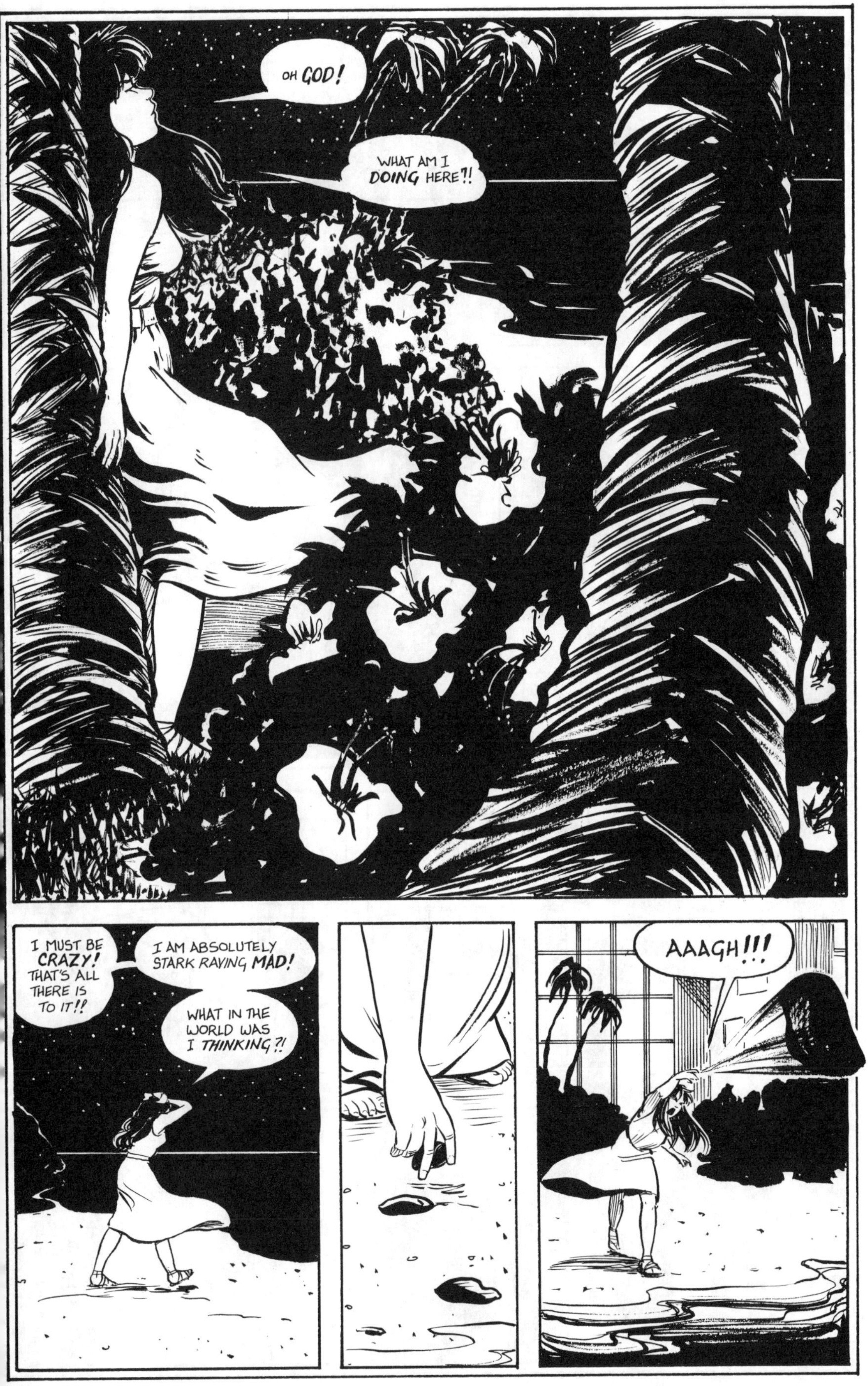
OH GOD!
WHAT AM I DOING HERE?!
I MUST BE CRAZY! THAT'S ALL THERE IS TO IT!!
I AM ABSOLUTELY STARK RAVING MAD!
WHAT IN THE WORLD WAS I THINKING?!
AAAGH!!!

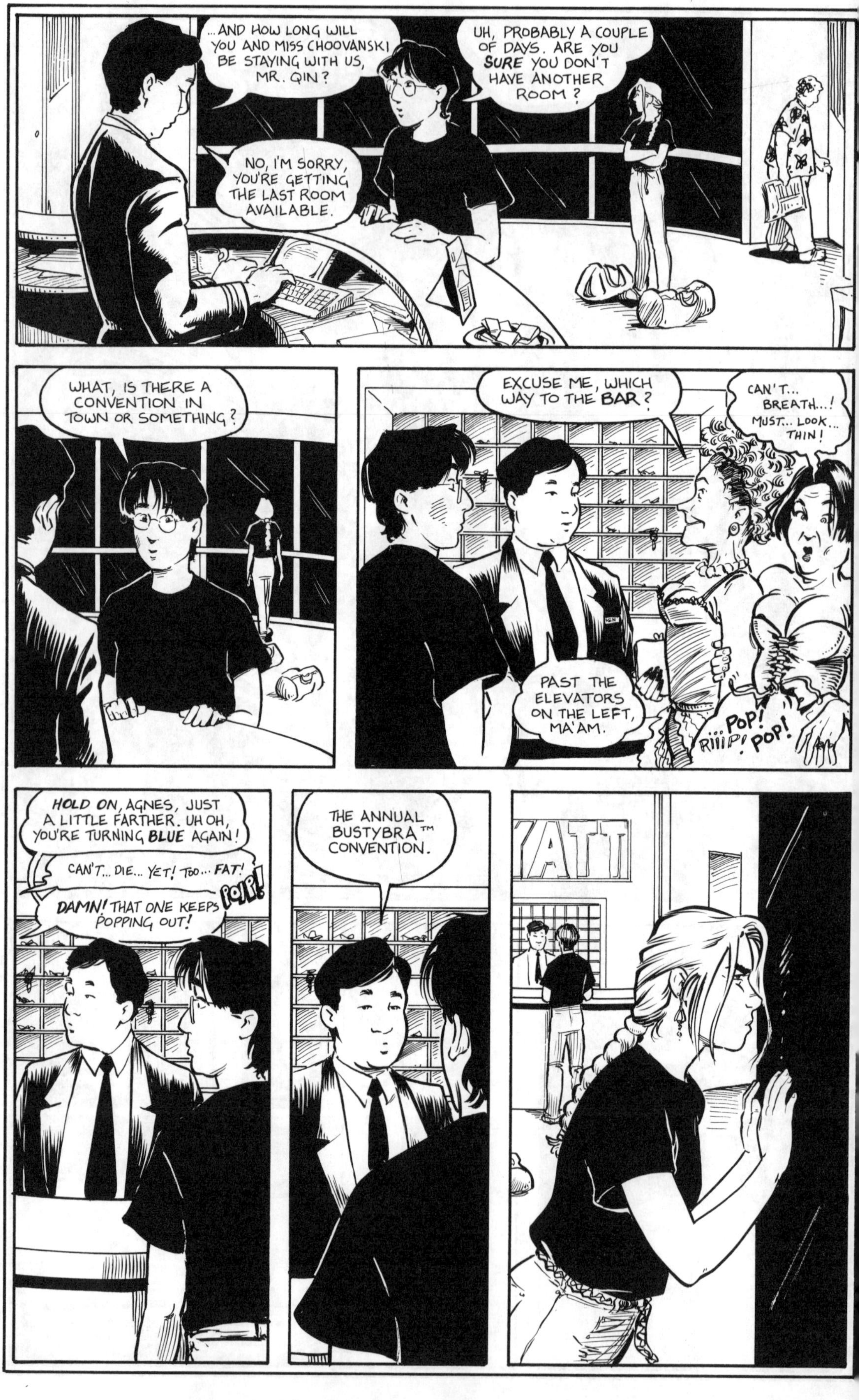
...AND HOW LONG WILL YOU AND MISS CHOOVANSKI BE STAYING WITH US, MR. QIN?
UH, PROBABLY A COUPLE OF DAYS. ARE YOU SURE YOU DON'T HAVE ANOTHER ROOM?
NO, I'M SORRY, YOU'RE GETTING THE LAST ROOM AVAILABLE.
WHAT, IS THERE A CONVENTION IN TOWN OR SOMETHING?
EXCUSE ME, WHICH WAY TO THE BAR?
CAN'T... BREATH...! MUST... LOOK... THIN!
PAST THE ELEVATORS ON THE LEFT, MA'AM.
POP! RIIIP! POP!
HOLD ON, AGNES, JUST A LITTLE FARTHER. UH OH, YOU'RE TURNING BLUE AGAIN!
CAN'T... DIE... YET! TOO... FAT!
DAMN! THAT ONE KEEPS POPPING OUT!
POP!
THE ANNUAL BUSTYBRA™ CONVENTION.

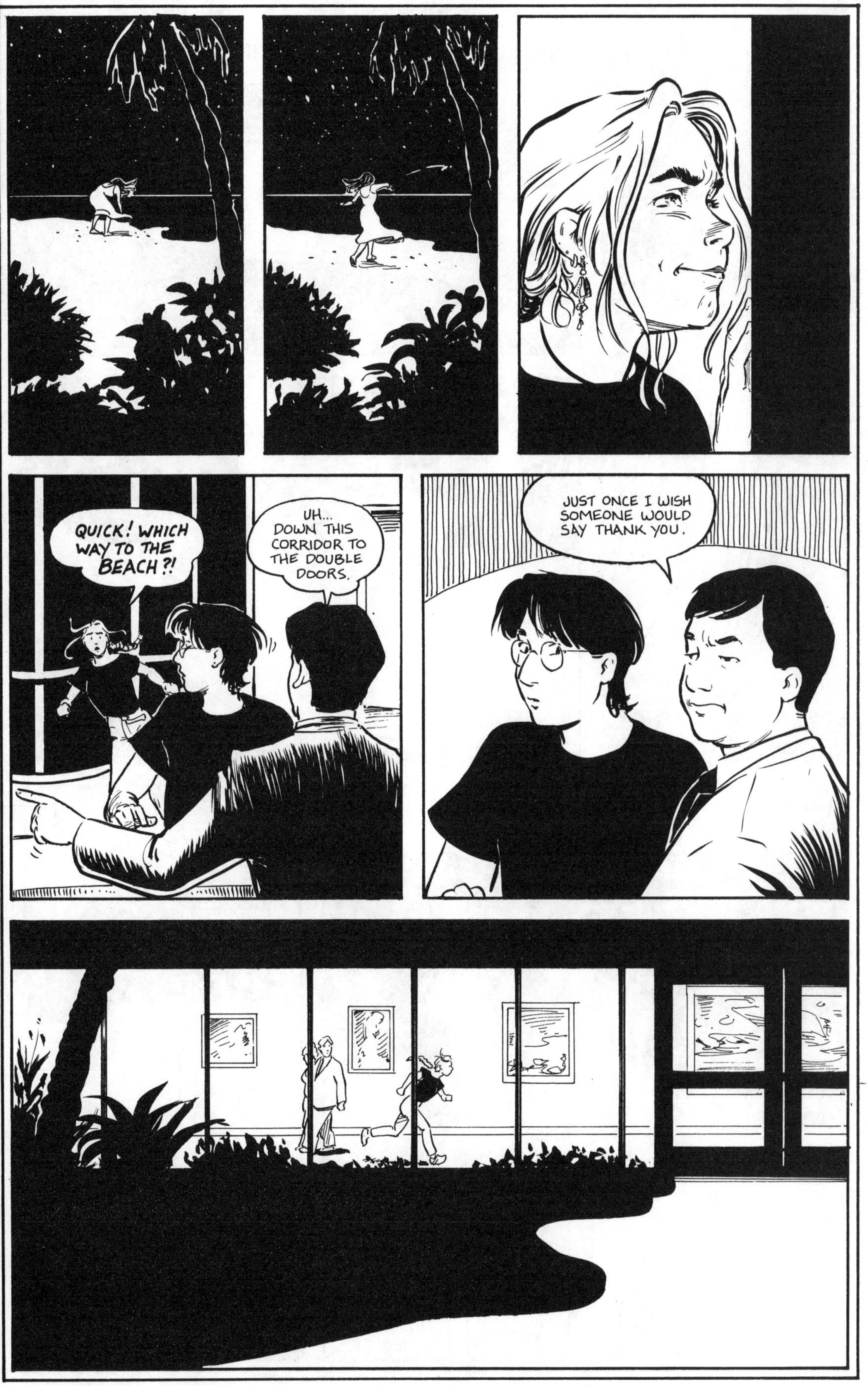
QUICK! WHICH WAY TO THE BEACH?!
UH... DOWN THIS CORRIDOR TO THE DOUBLE DOORS.
JUST ONCE I WISH SOMEONE WOULD SAY THANK YOU.

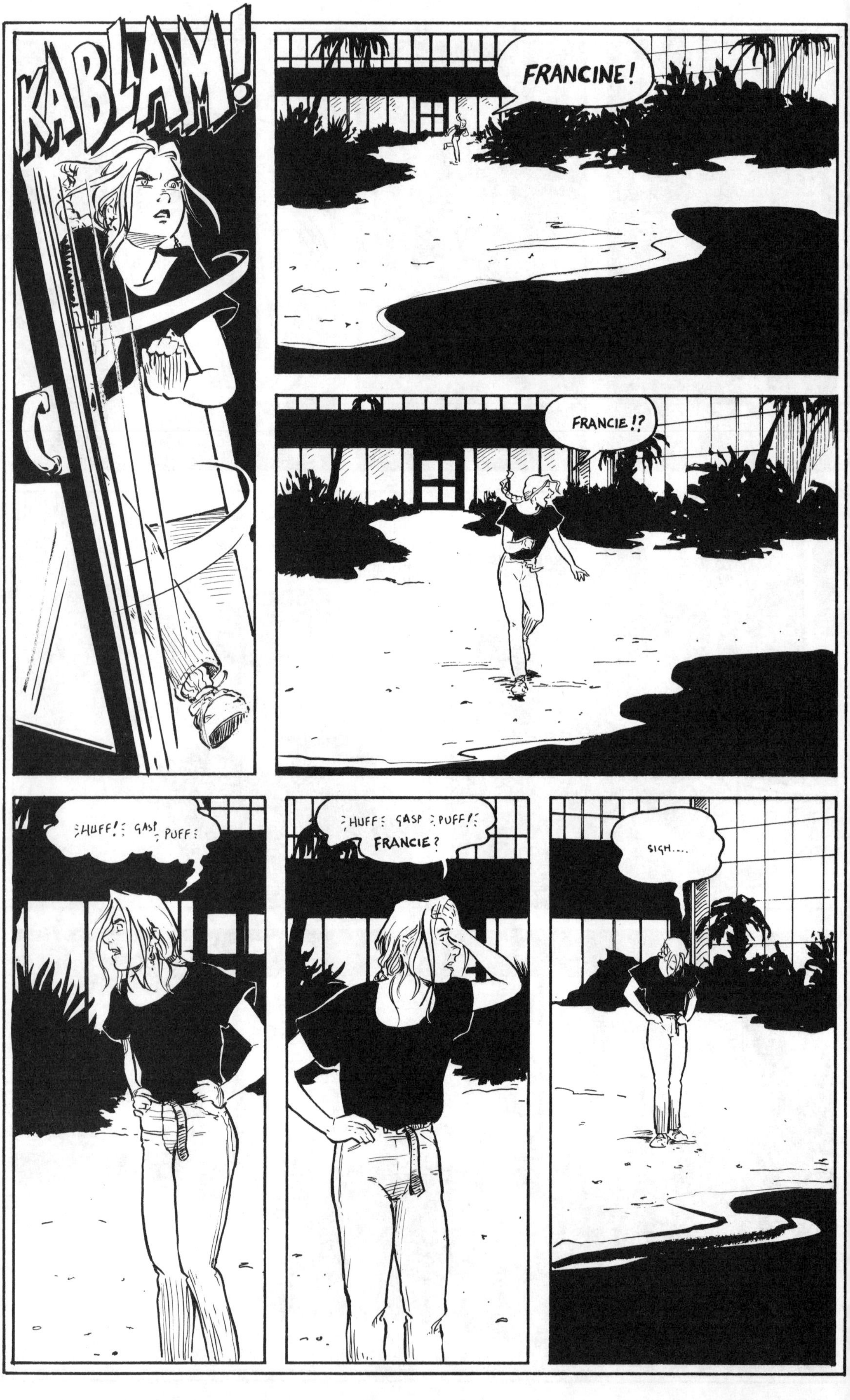
KABLAM!
FRANCINE!
FRANCIE!?
HUFF! GASP PUFF
HUFF GASP PUFF!
FRANCIE?
SIGH....

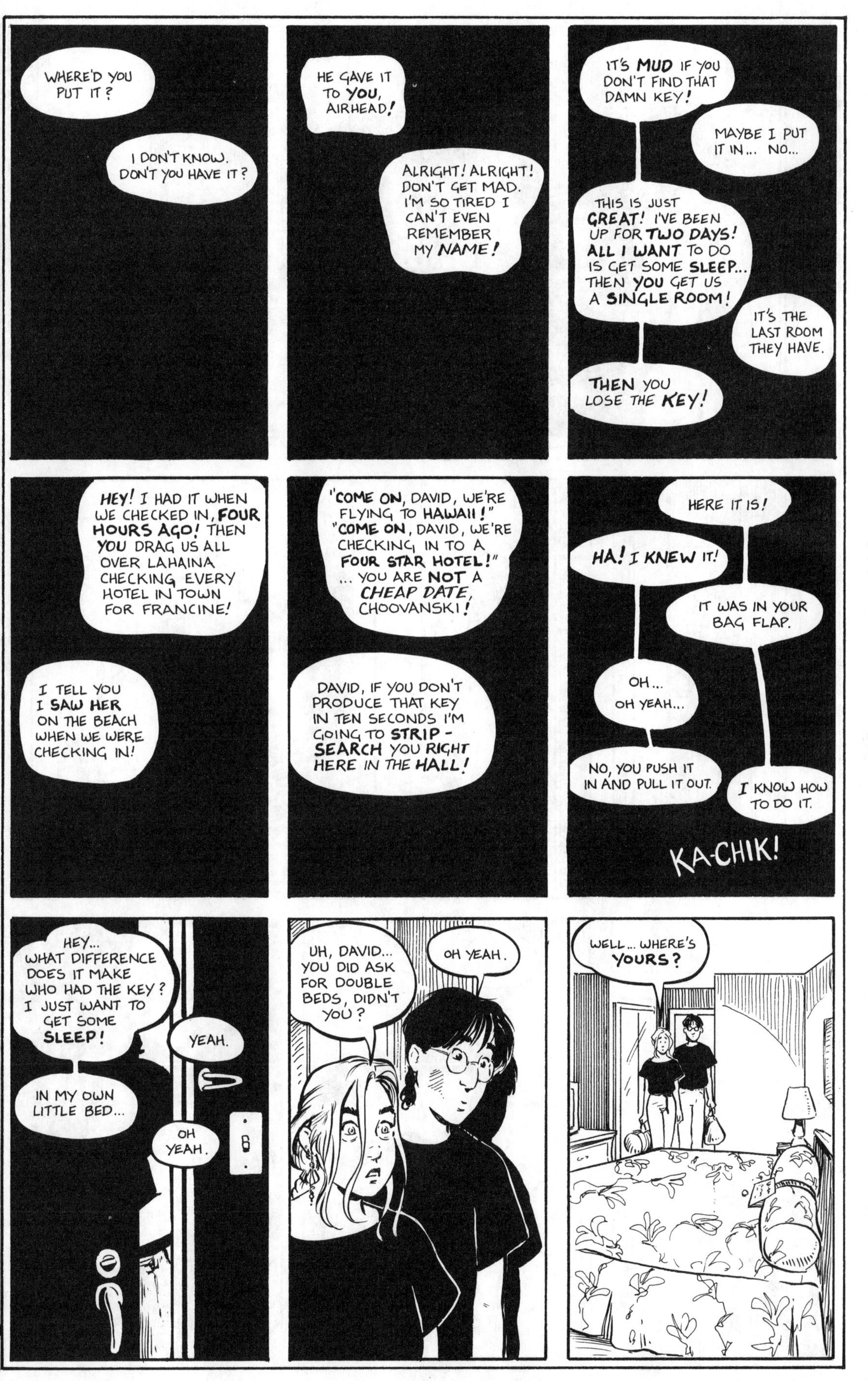

WHERE'D YOU PUT IT?
I DON'T KNOW. DON'T YOU HAVE IT?
HE GAVE IT TO YOU, AIRHEAD!
ALRIGHT! ALRIGHT! DON'T GET MAD. I'M SO TIRED I CAN'T EVEN REMEMBER MY NAME!
IT'S MUD IF YOU DON'T FIND THAT DAMN KEY!
MAYBE I PUT IT IN... NO...
THIS IS JUST GREAT! I'VE BEEN UP FOR TWO DAYS! ALL I WANT TO DO IS GET SOME SLEEP... THEN YOU GET US A SINGLE ROOM!
IT'S THE LAST ROOM THEY HAVE.
THEN YOU LOSE THE KEY!
HEY! I HAD IT WHEN WE CHECKED IN, FOUR HOURS AGO! THEN YOU DRAG US ALL OVER LAHAINA CHECKING EVERY HOTEL IN TOWN FOR FRANCINE!
I TELL YOU I SAW HER ON THE BEACH WHEN WE WERE CHECKING IN!
"COME ON, DAVID, WE'RE FLYING TO HAWAII!" "COME ON, DAVID, WE'RE CHECKING IN TO A FOUR STAR HOTEL!" ... YOU ARE NOT A CHEAP DATE, CHOOVANSKI!
DAVID, IF YOU DON'T PRODUCE THAT KEY IN TEN SECONDS I'M GOING TO STRIP-SEARCH YOU RIGHT HERE IN THE HALL!
HERE IT IS!
HA! I KNEW IT!
IT WAS IN YOUR BAG FLAP.
OH... OH YEAH...
NO, YOU PUSH IT IN AND PULL IT OUT.
I KNOW HOW TO DO IT.
KA-CHIK!
HEY... WHAT DIFFERENCE DOES IT MAKE WHO HAD THE KEY? I JUST WANT TO GET SOME SLEEP!
YEAH.
IN MY OWN LITTLE BED...
OH YEAH.
UH, DAVID... YOU DID ASK FOR DOUBLE BEDS, DIDN'T YOU?
OH YEAH.
WELL... WHERE'S YOURS?

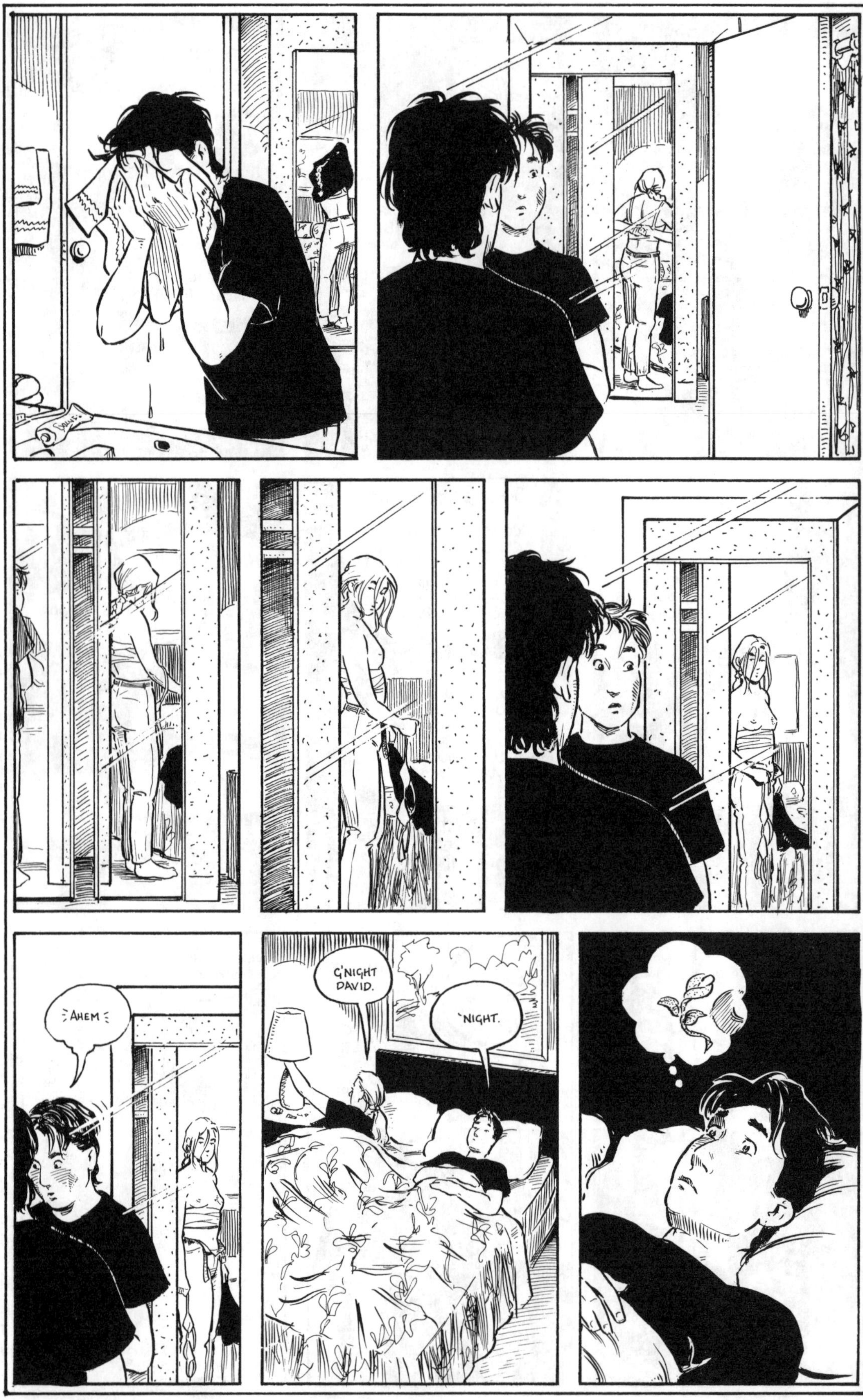
AHEM
G'NIGHT DAVID.
`NIGHT.

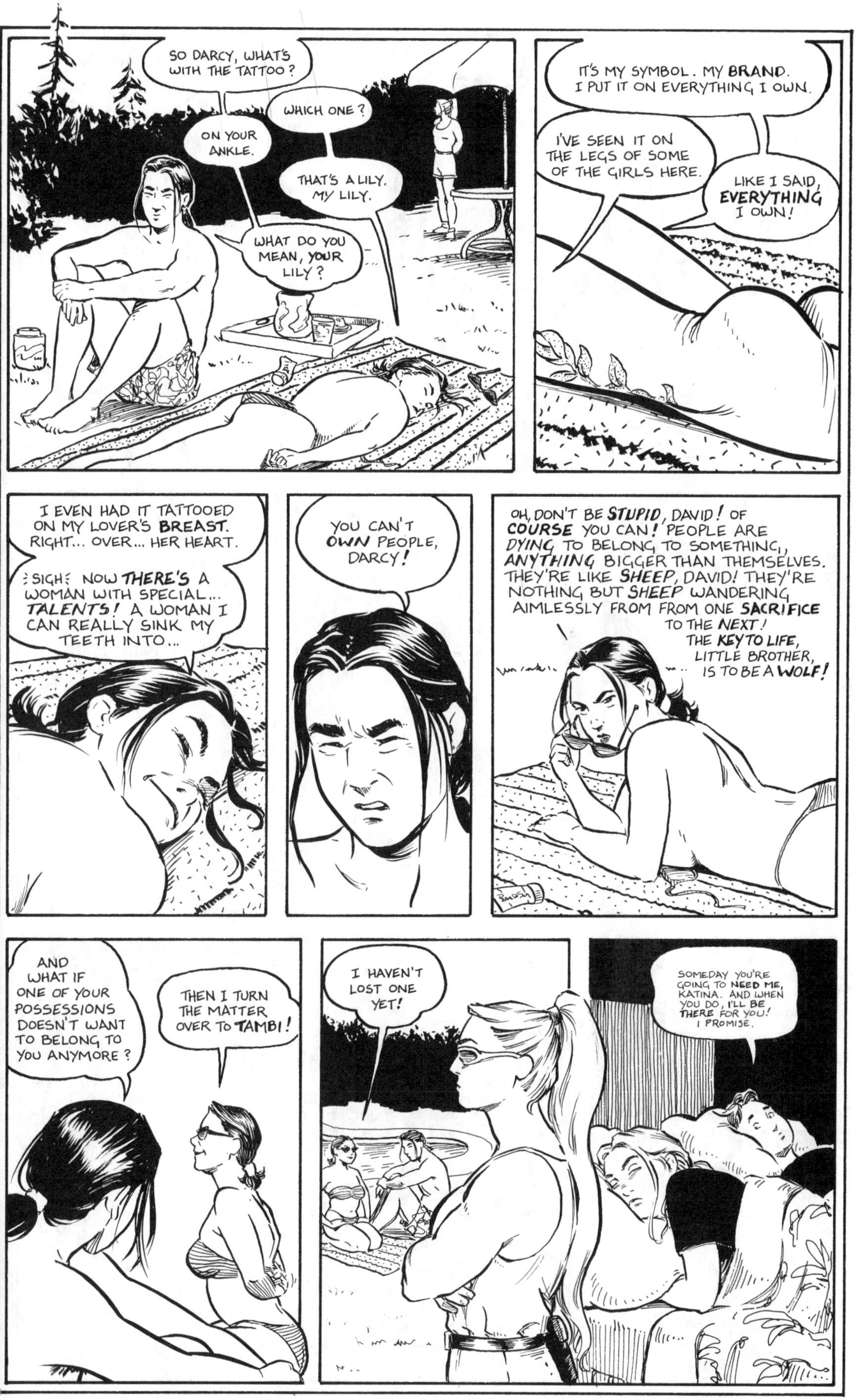
SO DARCY, WHAT'S WITH THE TATTOO?
WHICH ONE?
ON YOUR ANKLE.
THAT'S A LILY, MY LILY.
WHAT DO YOU MEAN, YOUR LILY?
IT'S MY SYMBOL. MY BRAND. I PUT IT ON EVERYTHING I OWN.
I'VE SEEN IT ON THE LEGS OF SOME OF THE GIRLS HERE.
LIKE I SAID, EVERYTHING I OWN!
I EVEN HAD IT TATTOOED ON MY LOVER'S BREAST. RIGHT... OVER... HER HEART.
SIGH NOW THERE'S A WOMAN WITH SPECIAL... TALENTS! A WOMAN I CAN REALLY SINK MY TEETH INTO...
YOU CAN'T OWN PEOPLE, DARCY!
OH, DON'T BE STUPID, DAVID! OF COURSE YOU CAN! PEOPLE ARE DYING TO BELONG TO SOMETHING, ANYTHING BIGGER THAN THEMSELVES. THEY'RE LIKE SHEEP, DAVID! THEY'RE NOTHING BUT SHEEP WANDERING AIMLESSLY FROM FROM ONE SACRIFICE TO THE NEXT! THE KEY TO LIFE, LITTLE BROTHER, IS TO BE A WOLF!
AND WHAT IF ONE OF YOUR POSSESSIONS DOESN'T WANT TO BELONG TO YOU ANYMORE?
THEN I TURN THE MATTER OVER TO TAMBI!
I HAVEN'T LOST ONE YET!
SOMEDAY YOU'RE GOING TO NEED ME, KATINA. AND WHEN YOU DO, I'LL BE THERE FOR YOU! I PROMISE.

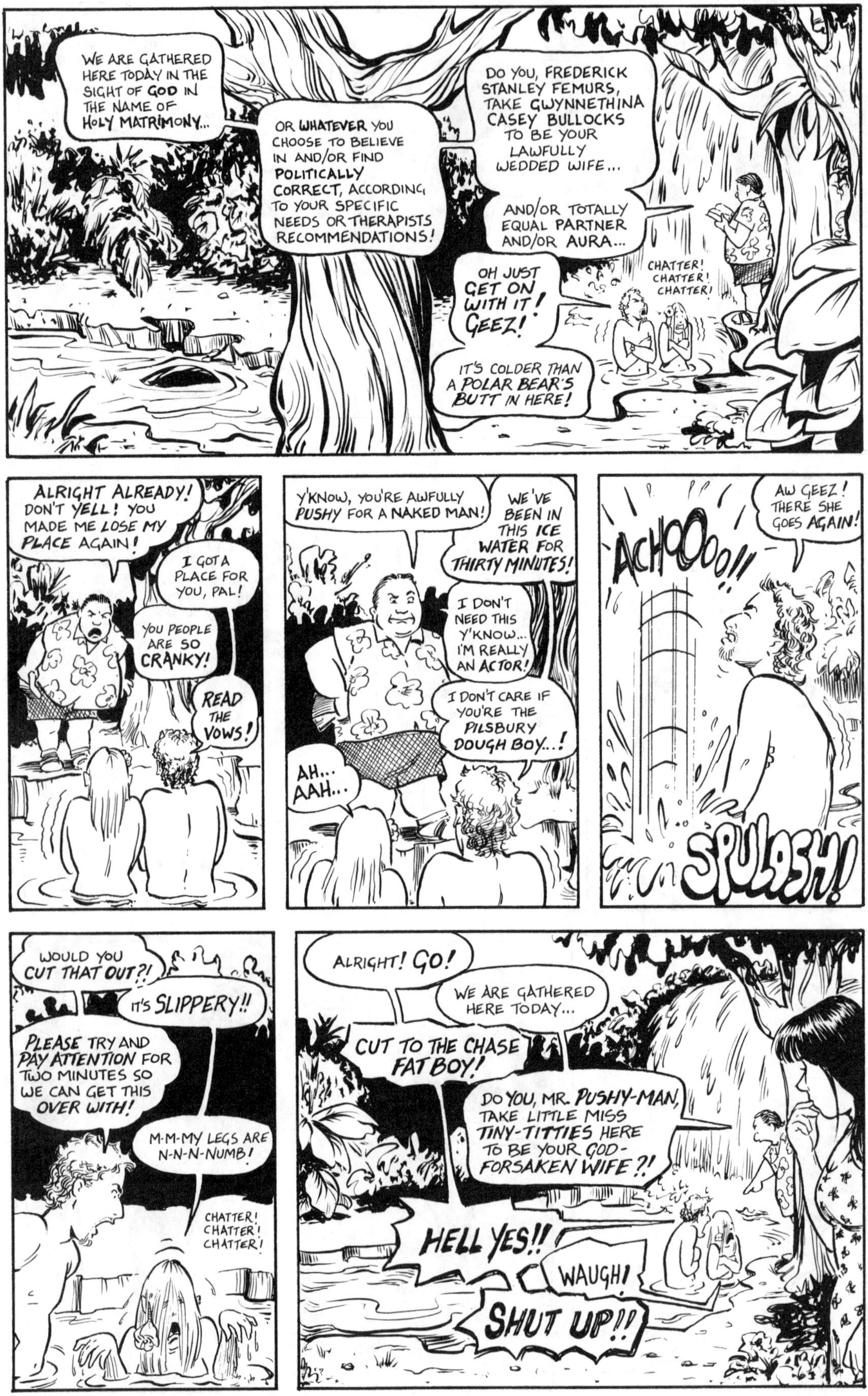
WE ARE GATHERED HERE TODAY IN THE SIGHT OF GOD IN THE NAME OF HOLY MATRIMONY...
OR WHATEVER YOU CHOOSE TO BELIEVE IN AND/OR FIND POLITICALLY CORRECT, ACCORDING TO YOUR SPECIFIC NEEDS OR THERAPISTS RECOMMENDATIONS!
DO YOU, FREDERICK STANLEY FEMURS, TAKE GWYNNETHINA CASEY BULLOCKS TO BE YOUR LAWFULLY WEDDED WIFE...
AND/OR TOTALLY EQUAL PARTNER AND/OR AURA...
CHATTER! CHATTER! CHATTER!
OH JUST GET ON WITH IT! GEEZ!
IT'S COLDER THAN A POLAR BEAR'S BUTT IN HERE!
ALRIGHT ALREADY! DON'T YELL! YOU MADE ME LOSE MY PLACE AGAIN!
I GOT A PLACE FOR YOU, PAL!
YOU PEOPLE ARE SO CRANKY!
READ THE VOWS!
Y'KNOW, YOU'RE AWFULLY PUSHY FOR A NAKED MAN!
WE'VE BEEN IN THIS ICE WATER FOR THIRTY MINUTES!
I DON'T NEED THIS Y'KNOW... I'M REALLY AN ACTOR!
I DON'T CARE IF YOU'RE THE PILSBURY DOUGH BOY...!
AH... AAH...
ACHOOOOO!!
AW GEEZ! THERE SHE GOES AGAIN!
SPULOSH!
WOULD YOU CUT THAT OUT?!
IT'S SLIPPERY!!
PLEASE TRY AND PAY ATTENTION FOR TWO MINUTES SO WE CAN GET THIS OVER WITH!
M-M-MY LEGS ARE N-N-N-NUMB!
CHATTER! CHATTER! CHATTER!
ALRIGHT! GO!
WE ARE GATHERED HERE TODAY...
CUT TO THE CHASE FAT BOY!
DO YOU, MR. PUSHY-MAN, TAKE LITTLE MISS TINY-TITTIES HERE TO BE YOUR GOD-FORSAKEN WIFE?!
HELL YES!!
WAUGH!
SHUT UP!!

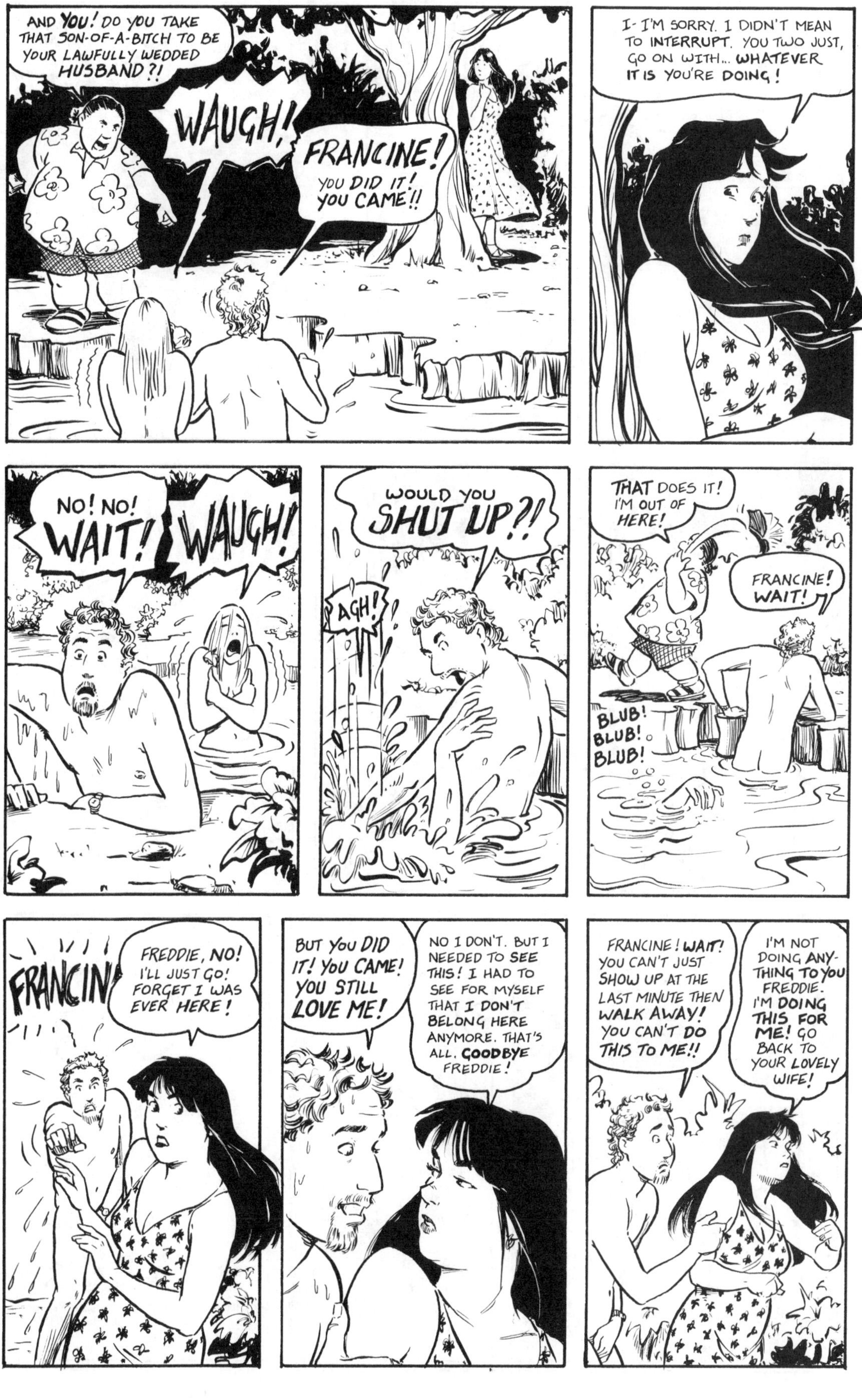
AND YOU! DO YOU TAKE THAT SON-OF-A-BITCH TO BE YOUR LAWFULLY WEDDED HUSBAND?!
WAUGH!
FRANCINE! YOU DID IT! YOU CAME!!
I- I'M SORRY. I DIDN'T MEAN TO INTERRUPT. YOU TWO JUST, GO ON WITH... WHATEVER IT IS YOU'RE DOING!
NO! NO! WAIT!
WAUGH!
WOULD YOU SHUT UP?!
AGH!
THAT DOES IT! I'M OUT OF HERE!
FRANCINE! WAIT!
BLUB! BLUB! BLUB!
FRANCIN
FREDDIE, NO! I'LL JUST GO! FORGET I WAS EVER HERE!
BUT YOU DID IT! YOU CAME! YOU STILL LOVE ME!
NO I DON'T. BUT I NEEDED TO SEE THIS! I HAD TO SEE FOR MYSELF THAT I DON'T BELONG HERE ANYMORE. THAT'S ALL. GOODBYE FREDDIE!
FRANCINE! WAIT! YOU CAN'T JUST SHOW UP AT THE LAST MINUTE THEN WALK AWAY! YOU CAN'T DO THIS TO ME!!
I'M NOT DOING ANY-THING TO YOU FREDDIE. I'M DOING THIS FOR ME! GO BACK TO YOUR LOVELY WIFE!

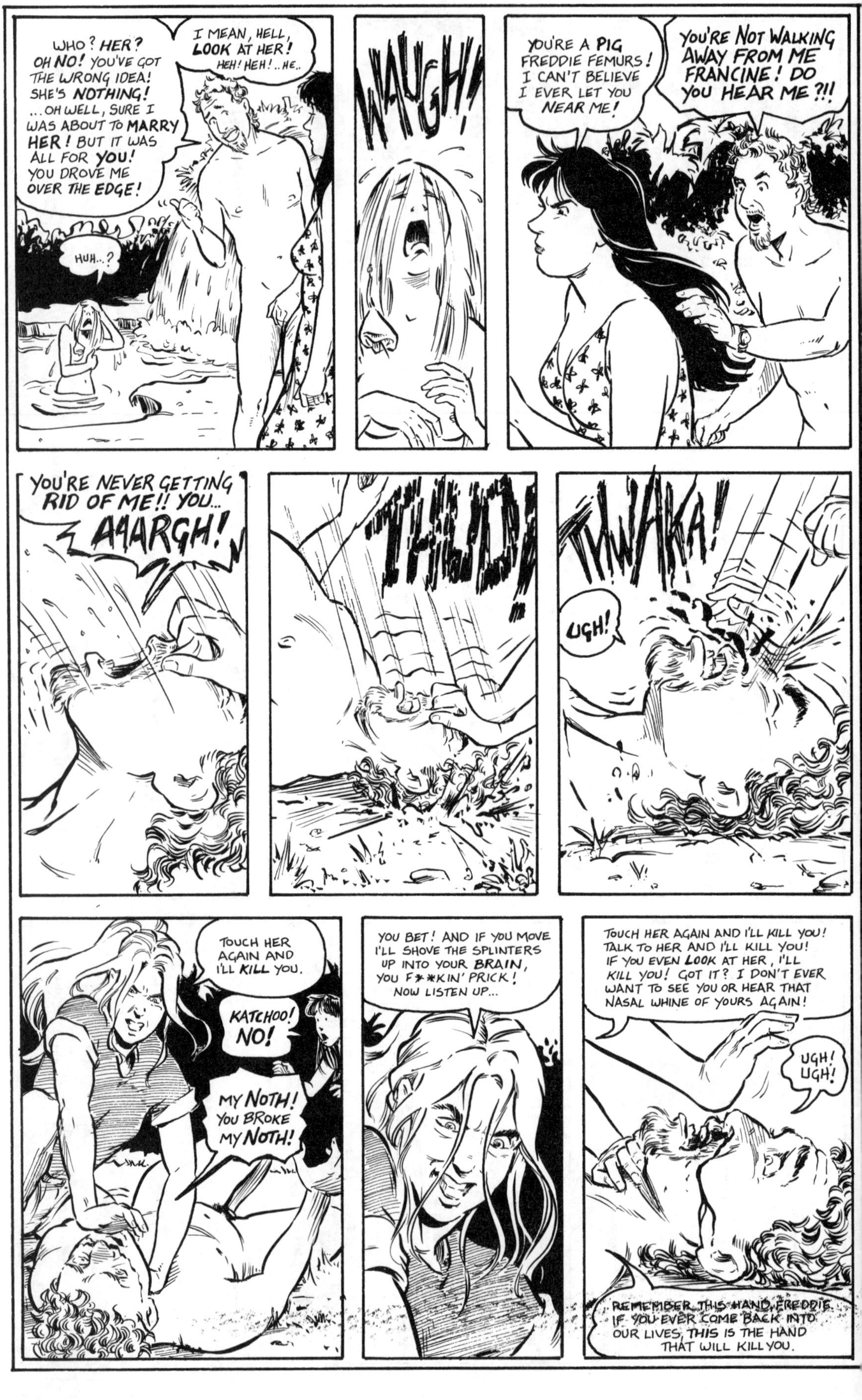

WHO? HER? OH NO! YOU'VE GOT THE WRONG IDEA! SHE'S NOTHING! ...OH WELL, SURE I WAS ABOUT TO MARRY HER! BUT IT WAS ALL FOR YOU! YOU DROVE ME OVER THE EDGE!
I MEAN, HELL, LOOK AT HER! HEH! HEH! .. HE..
HUH..?
WAUGH!!
YOU'RE A PIG FREDDIE FEMURS! I CAN'T BELIEVE I EVER LET YOU NEAR ME!
YOU'RE NOT WALKING AWAY FROM ME FRANCINE! DO YOU HEAR ME?!!
YOU'RE NEVER GETTING RID OF ME!! YOU... AAARGH!
THUD!
THWAKA!
UGH!
TOUCH HER AGAIN AND I'LL KILL YOU.
KATCHOO! NO!
MY NOTH! YOU BROKE MY NOTH!
YOU BET! AND IF YOU MOVE I'LL SHOVE THE SPLINTERS UP INTO YOUR BRAIN, YOU F**KIN' PRICK! NOW LISTEN UP...
TOUCH HER AGAIN AND I'LL KILL YOU! TALK TO HER AND I'LL KILL YOU! IF YOU EVEN LOOK AT HER, I'LL KILL YOU! GOT IT? I DON'T EVER WANT TO SEE YOU OR HEAR THAT NASAL WHINE OF YOURS AGAIN!
UGH! UGH!
REMEMBER THIS HAND, FREDDIE. IF YOU EVER COME BACK INTO OUR LIVES, THIS IS THE HAND THAT WILL KILL YOU.

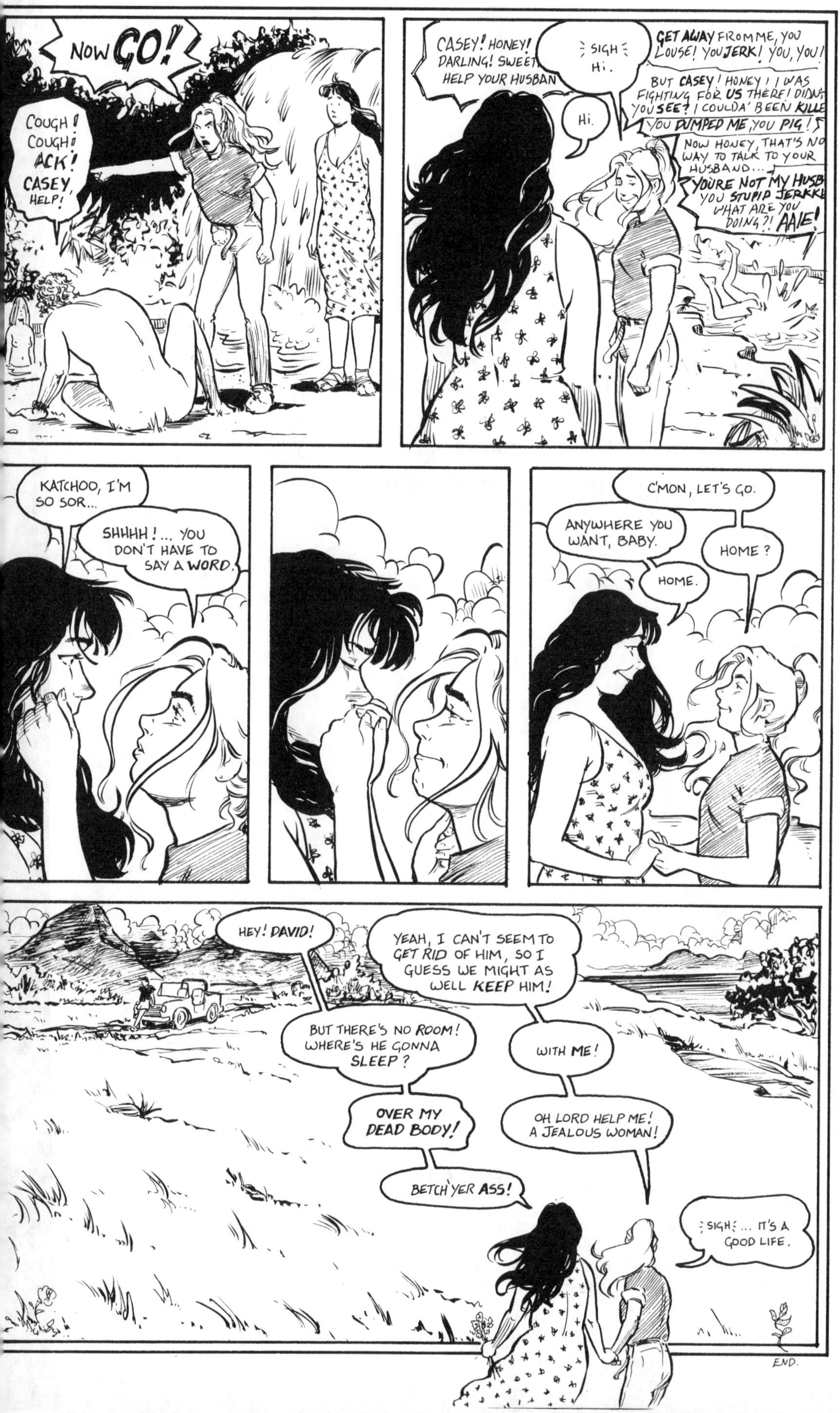
NOW GO!
COUGH! COUGH! ACK! CASEY, HELP!
CASEY! HONEY! DARLING! SWEET HELP YOUR HUSBAN
SIGH Hi.
Hi.
GET AWAY FROM ME, YOU LOUSE! YOU JERK! YOU, YOU!
BUT CASEY! HONEY! I WAS FIGHTING FOR US THERE! DIDN' YOU SEE? I COULDA' BEEN KILLE
YOU DUMPED ME, YOU PIG!
NOW HONEY, THAT'S NO WAY TO TALK TO YOUR HUSBAND...
YOU'RE NOT MY HUSB YOU STUPID JERKK WHAT ARE YOU DOING?! AAIE!
KATCHOO, I'M SO SOR...
SHHHH!... YOU DON'T HAVE TO SAY A WORD.
C'MON, LET'S GO.
ANYWHERE YOU WANT, BABY.
HOME?
HOME.
HEY! DAVID!
YEAH, I CAN'T SEEM TO GET RID OF HIM, SO I GUESS WE MIGHT AS WELL KEEP HIM!
BUT THERE'S NO ROOM! WHERE'S HE GONNA SLEEP?
WITH ME!
OVER MY DEAD BODY!
OH LORD HELP ME! A JEALOUS WOMAN!
BETCH'YER ASS!
SIGH ... IT'S A GOOD LIFE.
END.

Other fine books by Abstract Studio

The Collected Strangers In Paradise Vol. I
Strangers In Paradise (Vol II): I DREAM OF YOU
MOLLY & POO

Printed in Canada.

Strangers In Paradise is published by Abstract Studios, Inc. P.O. Box 271487, Houston, Texas 77277-1487, U.S.A.
EMail: SIPnet@AOL.COM All contents TM & ©1996 Terry Moore. The title, Strangers In Paradise and the likeness
of it's characters are trademarks of Terry Moore and their unauthorized use is prohibited by law and everything else we
can use to beat you to a bloody pulp if you try to rip them off. FOURTH PRINTING
ISBN: 1-892597-02-0